CRICUT MAKER 3 FOR BEGINNERS 2021

The Ultimate Guide to Master the New 2021 Cricut Maker 3 For Unique Crafts and Design

ESTEFANA SMITH

Copyright

Cricut Maker 3 for Beginners 2021

Copyright © 2021 Estefana Smith

All rights reserved. No part of this publication may be reproduced or transmitted in any form or by any means, electronic, or mechanical, including photocopying, recording, or by any information storage and retrieval system, without permission in writing from the publisher.

While the advice and information in this book are believed to be true and accurate at the date of publication, neither the authors nor the editors nor the publisher can accept any legal responsibility for any errors or omissions that may be made. The publisher makes no warranty, express or implied, with respect to the material contained herein.

Disclaimer

This book is geared towards providing information in regards to the topic and issue covered. The publication is sold with the idea that the publisher is not required to render accounting, officially permitted, or otherwise, qualified services. If advice is necessary. Legal or health professional, a practiced individual in the profession should be ordered.

Printed on acid-free paper.

Table of Contents

Copyright i
INTRODUCTION 1
CHAPTER ONE 4
What is a Cricut Machine? 4
How Does a Cricut Machine work? 4
The Cricut Maker 3 6
Features of Cricut Maker 3 and How to Use Them 8
How to Use a Cricut Maker 3 11
What Can I do with a Cricut Machine? 12
CHAPTER TWO 15
Types and Features of Cricut Cutting Machines 15
Cricut Explore 3 vs. Cricut Maker 3 17
CHAPTER THREE 20
How to Set Up Your Cricut Machine 20
Unboxing Your Cricut Maker 3 20
Familiarizing with Your Cricut Maker 3 Machine 22
Setting Up Your Cricut Maker 3 Machine 24
Making Your First Cut 26
Using Bluetooth in Cricut Maker 3 27
Pairing the Machine with a Computer 29
Resetting the Cricut Maker 3 31

Finding the Current Version of Cricut Design Space 32

Finding the Current Version of Cricut Design Space for Windows 32

Finding the Current Version of Cricut Design Space for Android 33

Finding the Current Version of Cricut Design Space for iOS........ 33

Finding the Current Version of Cricut Design Space for Mac 34

Choosing Material Settings 34

Using a Custom Material Setting in Windows or Mac 35

Using a Custom Material Setting in Android or iOS 36

Custom Cut Settings of the Cricut Machine 36

How to Create a New Custom Material 38

Installing the Bluetooth Adapter to the Cricut Machine 40

CHAPTER FOUR 42

Tools and Accessories Needed to Work with Cricut Maker 3 42

Materials 47

Installing a Pen 49

Selecting Pens 50

Cricut Pen and Markers Products 51

Types of Cricut Pens... 52

Types of Cricut Pens (used on any series except Cricut Joy) 53

Types of Cricut Pens used with Cricut Joy 55

Specific Blades and Tools for Cricut Maker 3 56

How to Tell your Cricut Machine to Write and Draw 57

CHAPTER FIVE 59

Different Blades for Different Materials 59

How to Calibrate the Cricut Knife Blade 61

Changing the Blades of the Cricut Machine 62

How to Cut Lightweight and Heavyweight Materials 66

How to Cut Lightweight Materials 66

How to Cut Heavyweight Materials 67

How to clean Your Cricut Maker 3 and the Necessary Materials to be used 68

Materials that should be used for Cleaning the Cricut maker 69

How to Clean the Cricut Maker 70

How to Clean the Front Rod in the Cricut Maker 70

How to Clean the Cricut Blades in the Cricut Maker 71

How to Clean the Cricut Heat Press in the Cricut Maker 72

How to Clean the Mat in the Cricut Maker 73

Cleaning of the Clamps 74

Cleaning the Rear Rod 75

Cleaning the Outside of Your Cricut Machine 76

CHAPTER SIX 78

How to Design on Cricut Maker 3 78

Making Use of Sure Cuts A Lot 83

Features of Sure Cuts A Lot 85

Using Design Space 86

Top Panel of the Cricut Design Space 88

Undo and Redo 88

Operation 88

Material Colors 89

Select All or Deselect 89

Edit 89

Offset 90

Align 90

Arrange 90

Flip 90

Size 91

Rotate 91

How to Download the Design Space 91

Cricut Design Space Top Menu 93

Uploading Images to Design Space 96

Spacing of Letters 97

How to Weld 98

How to Slice 99

How to Flatten 100

How to Attach 101

How to Group or Ungroup 102

How to duplicate designs on Cricut Design Space 103

How to Delete Uploaded Images from Cricut Design Space 104

How to Color Sync 105

v

Getting Started with Text 106

How to Edit Images in Cricut Design Space Using the Slice Tool 106

How to Access Special Characters 109

How to Add Accents to Fonts 109

How to Add Accents to Fonts 109

How to Add Flourishes to Fonts 110

How to Add a Degree Symbol to Text 111

How to Curve a Text 111

How to Make a Stencil 113

What You Can Make with Stencils 113

Materials Required to Make Stencils 114

Making Stencils with Your Cricut Machine 114

How to Use Contour 117

CHAPTER SEVEN 119

Vinyl for Cricut Projects 119

Vinyl Tricks 121

Using the Cricut Transfer Tape 121

How to Layer vinyl 123

Iron-on Wood Wall 125

Weeding iron-on Vinyl 126

Applying Iron-on Vinyl 126

Design Space Software Secrets and the Design Space App 127

CHAPTER EIGHT 131

Cricut Projects	131
Searching For a Project	131
Starting A New Project	132
Customized Umbrella (Mickey Mouse Design)	133
Dress Embellishments	135
Floral Vinyl Wall Decals	136
Acrylic Keychains	137
Wood Sign	138
Paper Flowers	140
Birthday Cake Topper	141
Leather Hair Accessories	143
Leather Journal cover	145
Curving Text for Tumblers	146
Glass Ornaments with Adhesive vinyl	147
Cricut Infusible Ink Mousepad	148
FAQs	148
CONCLUSION	151
ABOUT THE AUTHOR	153

INTRODUCTION

Apart from paper projects, Cricut cutting machines are used by many for crafts on customized mugs, t-shirts, vinyl decals, and many more, which are then sold online or at other places. Cricut cutting machines cut so well, even intricate designs, that they make a beginner in crafts looks so professional. Aside School projects, exhibitions and personal use, you can start making money by owning and using your Cricut machine, particularly the Cricut Maker 3.

The Cricut Maker 3 is the latest model in the Cricut cutting machines family. It was released in June 2021, together with Cricut Explore 3. You need a powerful cutting machine for commercial purposes; the Cricut Maker 3 is exactly what you need. The Cricut Maker 3 is the king of smart cutting machine. The versatility, precision and performance are arguably the best for now; and it brings the craft workshop to you at home and everywhere you go.

In case you are new to Cricut cutting machines, there are older Cricut models –the Cricut Explore, Cricut Explore One and Cricut Explore Air. These old models are discontinued, but there are people who are still proud owners of them. The Cricut Design Space software or app continues to give support to them. The newly released Cricut Maker 3 and Cricut Explore 3 are replacing all older Cricut machines. The portable Cricut Joy has also been added to the present crops of Cricut cutting machines.

However, other older legacy models such as the Expression and Gypsy are no longer enjoying support from Cricut, and do not work with the Cricut Design Space software or app. This sets of machine use design cartridges anyway.

There is another older manual die-cutting Cricut cutting machine called the Cricut Cuttlebug. It has also been discontinued and no longer enjoys support from Cricut.

The Cricut Joy on the other hand is the most portable of the current 3 Cricut cutting machines. The Maximum cutting width of Cricut Joy is 5.5 inches. It is basically meant for smaller projects like stickers, greeting cards, labels and so on. It is also an ideal cutting machine for introducing anyone to Cricut machines.

The Cricut Explore 3 is a very good machine. It cuts more 100 materials ranging from vinyl, ironn-on, cardstock, bonded fabric, cork, papers. It cuts up to 12 inches in width, maximum. It however does not cut wood or loads of fabrics.

The Cricut Maker 3 however, can do all the Cricut Explore 3 can do and much more. It is faster and versatile, being able to cut wood, leather, crepe paper, and fabrics for sewing. The Cricut has a unique adaptive tool system. It has a rotary tool that can delicately and precisely cut fabrics just as designed and measured. There is no Cricut Maker 2. Cricut Maker 3 is intentionally named to meet up with number in the Explore series. The Cricut Maker 3 is the king of cutting machine, no doubt. It cuts fastest, has strongest motor, has the strongest cutting force, versatile tools, and can cut materials up to 12 feet without the mat.

The Cricut Maker 3 is sold officially at $399.99 on Cricut's website. It is costlier than the Cricut Explore 3, which is obtainable at the rate of $299.99 for one. Looking at the features and the capabilities of the Cricut Maker 3, the price tag in comparison with Cricut Explore 3, is reasonable. However, you can also buy any of the Cricut Machines in bundle form, that is additional materials will come with it. Depending on the quantities of materials, the bundle price ranges from $459.99 to $499.99. Additional tools for cutting, drawing, debossing, engraving and so on, can also be purchased separately with price ranging from $30 to $50 each. Cricut's Smart Materials can also be bought from the Cricut's official website and Amazon's.

This guide will put you through steps to take to make the best of your Cricut Maker 3.

CHAPTER ONE

What is a Cricut Machine?

Cricut machines are die-cutters or craft plotters used by handcrafters, creatives or just about anyone who works with materials and need to cut them to desired shapes. Cricut machines are electronic cutting machines used to cut designs from several types of materials in more precise and faster way than could be achieved manually with hand using scissors or knife. Cricut Machines can cut materials such as paper, cotton, silk, vinyl, card stock, iron-on transfers, and even denim, leather and wood.

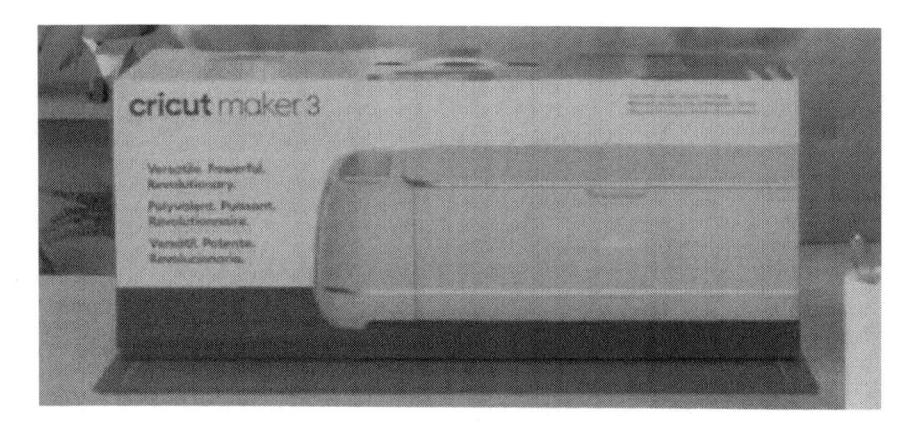

How Does a Cricut Machine work?

Cricut machines look like a printer, and can be mistaken for it. Rather than printing on the materials, they use their precise blades to cut them according to the designs fed to them.

Well, the designs are created using a software or app after which the designs are sent to the cutting machines through USB port or Bluetooth. When the Cricut Machine receives the design, it cuts precisely as instructed.

There are three types of Cricut cutting machines: the Cricut Maker 3, The Cricut Explore 3, and the Cricut Joy.

Cricut Joy is the most affordable of the Cricut cutting machines. It is more portable and easy to set up, but has minimal capacity. It is intended for minor on-the-go tasks. Cricut Explore 3 is an average and popular machine, but the Cricut Maker 3 is a higher spec of it, which can cut a wider range of materials and uses more tools.

It is very easy to use any Cricut cutting machine. Ensure to press the power button of your machine; then follow the steps below to use your Cricut cutting machine:

>**Step 1:** Load the cutting mat into the Cricut machine. The mat is sticky, to hold the material in place.

>**Step 2:** Then go to your software or app, Cricut Design Space, on your device to select a design. Adjust material settings there.

>**Step 3:** Send the design to the Cricut cutting machine either through Bluetooth or USB cable.

>**Step 4:** Thereafter, press the button on your Cricut cutting machine to start cutting.

Step 5: The Cricut machine will start cutting. When it is done, you can now remove the material from the mat.

The Cricut Maker 3

The Cricut Maker 3 is synonymous with smartness, fastness, and strength when it comes to modern craft-plotting or die-cutting machines. It is smarter, faster and stronger than all previous models and even new ones. It is a must-have for any craft professional or hobbyist.

It can cut more than 300 types of materials ranging from paper to heavy chipboard. Cricut sells its own materials, which it calls Smart Materials. These materials can easily be fed into the machine without the cutting mat. Cricut Maker 3 will cut smart materials twice as fast as the older model. Using Smart Materials also cuts down waste when you are trying to cut your other materials to fit into the cutting mat.

There are only 3 types of Smart Materials available – Smart Vinyl, Smart Paper Sticker Cardstock and Smart Iron-on.

Cricut Maker 3 cuts Smart Materials up to 12 feet (3.6m) without a cutting mat. It is possible to cut materials up to 330mm wide and 3,600mm long if a roll holder is used. The roll holder is sold separately - at about $50. Basically, the type of material will tell on the cutting length that can be attained.

You can switch the tool head from one tool to another. The tool clamps are labelled **A** and **B**, and you can do two things at the same time such as cutting and writing. It has 13 tools with different functions to - score, write, cut, deboss, engrave or add embellishments with decorative materials with professional precision. Cricut Maker 3 is more than ten times stronger when cutting than the Cricut Explore series.

It uses Design space apps, which are available on PCs, smart phones, tablets and other smart devices using any of the following operating systems – Android, Windows, iOS, and Mac. Connectivity with these devices is either through Bluetooth or through USB. The software or app is free.

There is a subscription service called Cricut Access, which can be either Premium or Standard. The Premium subscription is only available on a yearly payment basis and it costs $120, while the payment for Standard subscription can be made either on a monthly or yearly basis. Standard subscription annual fee is $96, but if you opt for monthly subscription, it is $ 10 only. Both Premium and Standard subscriptions give access to over 500 fonts, over 150,000 images and Thousands of ready to use projects. In the case of licensed images, you get a 10% discount when you purchase. However, with Premium subscription you get 20% discount on purchases on Cricut website (cricut.com) and get free economy shipping if your orders are worth $50 or more.

Features of Cricut Maker 3 and How to Use Them

The Cricut Maker 3 is similar to the older model. It is compact and looks a lot like a printer. The machine has an under-tray slot for keeping tool heads. It also has a storage area for keeping other tool pieces. It will fit well on a work desk or computer table in homes, offices, workshops and other places without taking too much space or causing an issue.

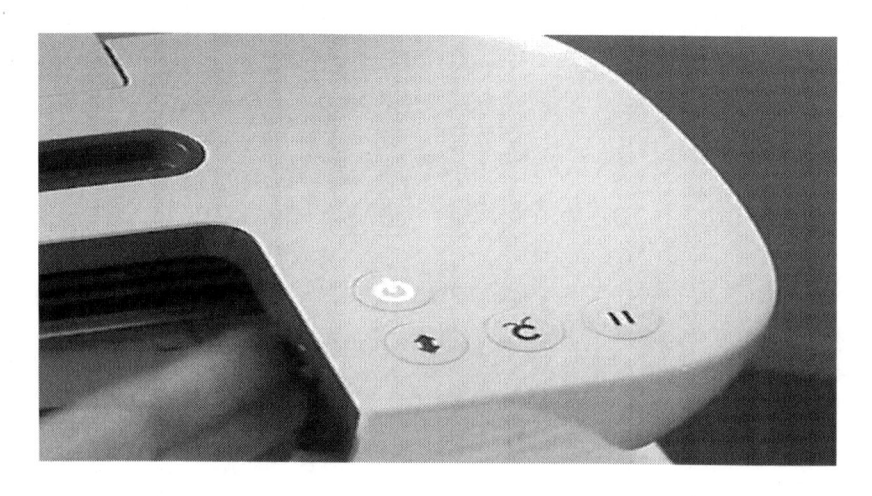

Unlike in the older Maker model where the symbol for the power button is **C**, the Cricut Maker 3 replaces that with the universal power button. The power adapter gives a 3 Amps output that enables Cricut Maker 3 to boast of the capability to deliver 10 times the cutting force of the Explore machine series. Not only that, it enables faster speeds and cutting without the mat. It is also twice as fast as the older model.

The tool head clamps are labelled **A** and **B**. The Cricut Maker 3 is compatible with 13 tools, which can be used for writing, cutting, embellishing, scoring and foiling.

There are samples of Smart Materials with your purchase of a new Cricut Maker 3. You might need to purchase more, but the samples will give you a feel of the Smart Materials; and how awesome they are to use without you cutting them to fit into a cutting mat.

To ensure a straight edge after each cut, there is an in-built trimmer that does that. The trimmer in Cricut Maker 3 is an upgrade from the previous model, having a little over 13 inches, and bigger. This will allow it to accommodate Smart Materials, which are 13 inches wide, and other larger materials.

The roll holder, which does not come with a purchase of the Cricut Maker 3, is the additional feature or tool which will make working with larger Smart Materials rolls easy and aligned for a smooth and successful project. It has the capacity to hold up to 75 ft (22.8 m) roll.

The amazing Cricut Maker 3 can cut more than 300 types of materials. It can cut silk, cotton, paper, mat board, leather, vinyl and so on. It has a superb rotary blade that cuts almost any fabric. Knife blade can be used with it to cut even thicker materials up to 2.4 mm.

The Cricut Maker 3 also has scoring wheels used for creating crisp folds and razor-sharp creases. For embellishments, the foil transfer tool is handy.

There are other tools for engraving, debossing and creating other decorative effects. Cricut Maker has Bluetooth wireless technology, which connects to a laptop or desktop computer wirelessly. It also connects using USB port for projects. The USB port can be used for charging other devices.

The Cricut Maker 3 uses the free Cricut Design Space app (on both iOS and Android) and Cricut Design Space application (on Windows and Mac) to send a design to your Cricut machine. The app or software has numerous ready-to-use designs, which you can quickly make use of. You can also create your own.

How to Use a Cricut Maker 3

A PC or a smartphone is required to gain access to Cricut's design software and send your design to the Cricut cutting machine – either Windows or Mac. The Cricut Explore 3 and Cricut Maker 3 can connect to a laptop or desktop computer via USB cable or wirelessly via Bluetooth. The Cricut Joy connects via Bluetooth only. You can also use the Cricut Design Space app (on both iOS and Android) to send a design to your Cricut machine from your smartphone.

It is very easy to use any Cricut Maker 3 machine. Follow these simple steps below to use it:

Step 1: Load the cutting mat into your Cricut Maker 3.

Step 2: Connect your machine to a power socket and press the power button on your machine to put it on.

Step 3: Then go to your software or app, Cricut Design Space, on your device to select a design. Ensure to adjust material settings there.

Step 4: Send the design to your Cricut Maker 3 cutting machine either through Bluetooth or USB cable.

Step 5: Thereafter, press the button on your Cricut Maker 3 machine to start cutting.

Step 6: The Cricut Maker 3 machine will start cutting. When it is done, you can now remove the material from the mat.

This guide however will elaborate on the above, discuss various settings, benefits and mention how to use the tools and accessories with many tips to make you have a stress-free experience using the amazing Cricut Maker 3.

What Can I do with a Cricut Machine?

Cricut cutting machines are for everyone, but much more for the creatives and craft professionals and students. There is almost no limit to what you can use the machine for. The only known limitation is your imagination. Cricut machines can cut even the most intricate design quietly and faster than would have been done manually.

Iron-on is what will make you use an iron to stick a material to a fabric such as the t-shirt, handkerchiefs, bags, hats and so on. The resulting projects are usually long lasting. Iron-on vinyls are also known as Heat Transfer Vinyl (HTV).

Cricut machines mainly cut, but it also writes and draws. You can also use it to score, embellish, deboss, engrave and so on.

Amongst the several things a Cricut cutting machine can be used for, a few are thus mentioned:

- Paper flyers
- Party decorations
- Greeting cards
- Leather bracelets
- Vinyl decals
- Monograms for mugs
- Stickers
- Arts projects
- Signs
- Sewing patterns
- Balsa wood cuts
- Christmas tree ornaments
- Quilts
- Fabric cuts
- Jigsaw puzzles
- Jewelry making
- Wedding invites
- Business cards
- Baby clothes
- Calligraphy signs
- Headbands
- Gift tags
- Price tags
- Hanging cork board
- Pet clothes
- Socks

- Stencils
- Iron-on for t-shirts, handkerchiefs and other fabrics
- And many more.

CHAPTER TWO

Types and Features of Cricut Cutting Machines

Presently, there are three types of Cricut machines: **the Cricut Maker 3, the Cricut Explore 3 and the Cricut Joy.** The Cricut Maker 3 replaces all the older Maker series, while the Cricut Explore 3 replaces all the older Explorer series. The Cricut Joy machine however is recently released as the baby of the Cricut machine family, being neither a Maker nor Explore brand. It is portable and intended for smaller scale projects.

There are, however, older Cricut models – the Cricut Explore, Cricut Explore One and Cricut Explore Air. These old models are discontinued, but there are people who are still proud owners of them, most especially the popular Cricut Explore Air 2. The Cricut Design Space software or app continues to give support to them.

However, other older legacy models, which use design cartridges, such as the Expression and Gypsy, are no longer enjoying support from Cricut. They also do not work with the Cricut Design Space software or app.

There is another older manual die-cutting Cricut cutting machine called the Cricut Cuttlebug. It has also been discontinued and no longer enjoys support from Cricut.

Let's look at the most recent types of Cricut cutting machines and their features:

The Cricut Joy is the most portable of the current three Cricut cutting machines. The Maximum cutting width of Cricut Joy is 5.5 inches. It is basically meant for smaller projects like stickers, greeting cards, labels and so on. It is also an ideal cutting machine for introducing anyone to Cricut machines.

The Cricut Explore 3 is a very good machine. It cuts more than 100 materials ranging from vinyl, iron-on, cardstock, bonded fabric, cork, and papers. It cuts up to 12 inches in width, maximum. It however does not cut wood or loads of fabrics.

The Cricut Maker 3, on the other hand, can do all the Cricut Explore 3 can do and much more. It is faster and versatile: being able to cut wood, leather, crepe paper, and fabrics for sewing. The Cricut Maker 3 has a rotary tool that can delicately and precisely cut fabrics just as designed and measured. The Cricut Maker 3 is the king of cutting machines, no doubt. It cuts fastest, has the strongest motor, has the strongest cutting force, versatile tools, and can cut materials up to 12 feet without the mat.

Cricut Explore 3 vs. Cricut Maker 3

The major differences between the Cricut Explore 3 and the Cricut Maker 3, apart from their prices, are in strength and other features, which make the former looks like an upgrade of the earlier. With a small amount of money to add, buying the latest Cricut Maker 3, instead of the Cricut Explore 3, gives a kind of assurance, knowing that you have a super machine that can take care of most of your cutting jobs. Cricut Explore 3 is a powerful machine too. For the conveniences of the price and intention to use for less-heavier projects, the Cricut Explore 3 is just as good.

The Cricut Explore 3 can cut stabilized fabrics, cardboards, tooling feathers, stiffened felt, craft foam, natural wood veneer, and so on. It does not have the rotary cutting tools like the Cricut Maker 3. Therefore, you might need to use additional stabilizers, to come out with a successful cutting task. The Cricut Explore 3 has the Deep-point blade that enables it to cut thin wood veneer.

The Cricut Maker 3, on the other hand, can cut the widest range of materials, heavier materials inclusive. Basswood, balsa wood, plywood, heavy chipboard and so on are pieces of cake for the Cricut Maker 3. It has the rotary cutting tool and has no need for additional stabilizers.

The table below shows the comparison between the Cricut Explore 3 and the Cricut Maker 3 explicitly.

	Cricut Explore 3	**Cricut Maker 3**
Types of materials	More than 100	More than 300
Maximum material width	13 inches	13 inches
Maximum cut length	12 feet	12 feet
Types of tools	6	13
Tools	• Cutting • Writing	• Cutting • Writing

	• Scoring • Foiling	• Scoring • Debossing • Engraving • Foiling • And so on
Commercial Use	No	Yes
Cuts without cutting mat	Yes	Yes
Uses card mat	No	No
Connectivity	• USB • Bluetooth	• USB • Bluetooth
Works with printer to print and cut	Yes	Yes
Price range	$290 - $310	$390 - $410

CHAPTER THREE

How to Set Up Your Cricut Machine

When you purchase your new Cricut Maker 3, the first thing you want to do is to unbox it and crosscheck all the accessories are there. Then you should set it up. Setting it up will entail you connecting it to Cricut Design Space app or software and cutting your first test sticker using one of the Smart Materials that comes with it.

Unboxing Your Cricut Maker 3

When you take delivery of your Cricut Maker 3 cutting machine, open the box and follow the steps below:

Step 1: Remove the protective cardboards.

Step 2: You will see a sheet of Smart Paper Sticker Cardstock, Transfer Tape, Smart Iron-on, and Smart Vinyl. These samples are given so that you can try them out. If you love the conveniences they provide, then you can purchase more from Cricut web store or elsewhere.

Step 3: Then pull out the machine. Cricut Maker 3 is pre-loaded with Premium Fine Point Blade.

Step 4: Right under the machine you just pulled out, and still in the box, are the power adapter and the USB cable. Bring them out.

Step 5: Remove the plastic from the machine and also the Styrofoam from the tool housing and put them in the box. Put the box away.

Step 6: Put the machine on the desk or wherever you want it, and open the top of the machine by pulling it up.

Step 7: Plug the power adapter to the power socket.

However, if it is one of the bundles you bought, you should find additional numbers of Smart Materials and tools, depending on the bundle you purchased.

Basically, you should find the following items in your box:

1. Cricut Maker 3 machine pre-loaded with a Premium Fine Point Blade.
2. A welcome card
3. Adaptive tool housing
4. USB cable

5. Power adapter
6. Four sample Smart materials – Smart Vinyl, Smart Sticker Cardstock, Transfer Tape, and Smart Iron-on for practice cut.
7. A free trial subscription to Cricut Access for new subscribers
8. More than a hundred ready-to-use projects online.

Familiarizing with Your Cricut Maker 3 Machine

After you must have un-boxed your Machine as instructed in Section 3.1.1, you then need to proceed to set up your Cricut Maker 3 machine. However, before you do this, you need to familiarize yourself with the machine.

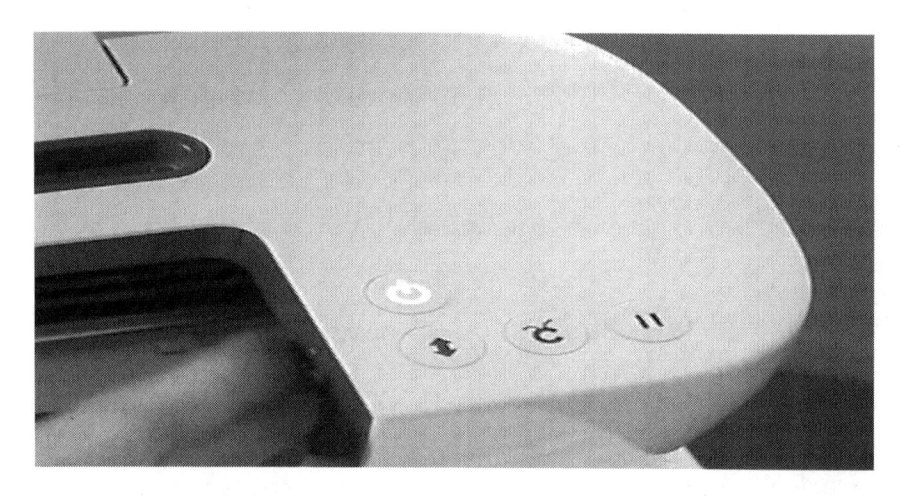

You will see four buttons on the right side of the machine. These buttons are the **power** button, **load and unload** button, **start** button and **pause** button.

The Cricut Maker 3 is pre-installed with the Premium Fine-Point Blade in the clamp labelled **B**. Pull it out of the clasp if you desire to swap it with another tool. Then put in the new tool and secure it back.

The clamp labelled **A** on the other hand is designed to hold markers, pens, or a scoring stylus.

There is also a silicone storage cup located on the left for storing tools and blades in. There is an additional storage under-tray at the bottom of the Cricut Maker 3 machine as well, where you can keep your hand tools, blades and other accessories.

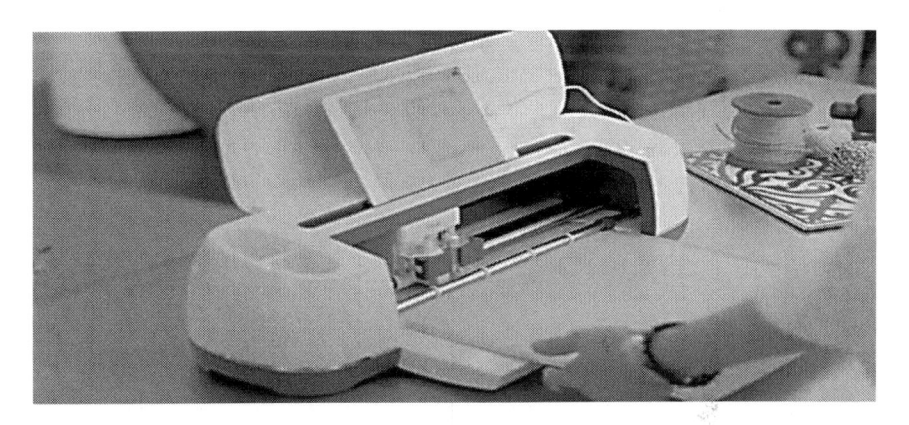

The Cricut Maker 3 has a place at the top of it to hold your device (smartphone or tablet) while using it or charging it. The machine has a USB port on the side, which can be used to charge your device.

At the back of the machine, plug in the power adapter into your Cricut Maker 3 machine and the other end into the power outlet. The power button is for putting on the machine.

Setting Up Your Cricut Maker 3 Machine

It is time to set up your Cricut Maker 3; follow the steps below, to do so:

Step 1: You need to download the Cricut Design Space. Go to **cricut.com/setup** from your device or PC.

Step 2: Click **Download**

Step 3: Locate **Cricut ID** and create an account for yourself.

Step 4: When an account has been created successfully, login into the Design Space software or app.

Step 5: Using Bluetooth or a USB cable, you will then need to connect your Cricut Maker 3 to your PC or device. Plug in your USB cable or turn on your Bluetooth on your device or PC to do so.

Step 6: Then click on **New Product Set-Up** on your Design Space

Step 7: Click **Smart Cutting Machine**

Step 8: Select **Maker 3.** If connection is by USB cable, select **Maker 3: 0 USB**

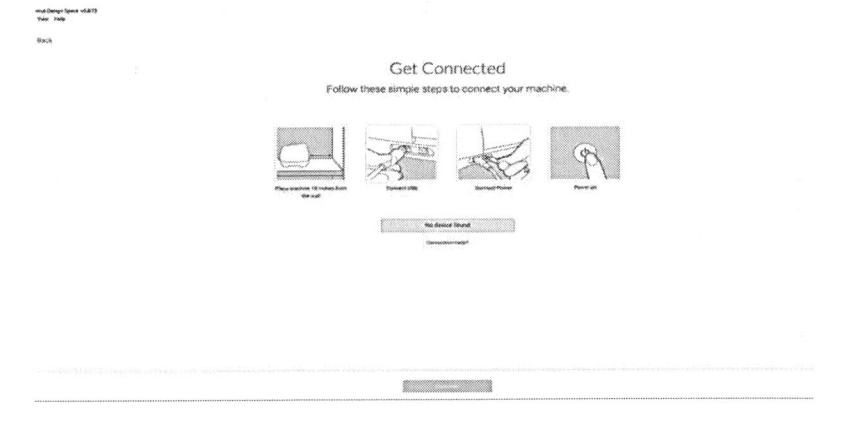

Step 9: Click **Continue**

Step 10: Follow the prompts afterwards. If you desire sign up for the free trial of Cricut Access, click **Start Free Trial**.

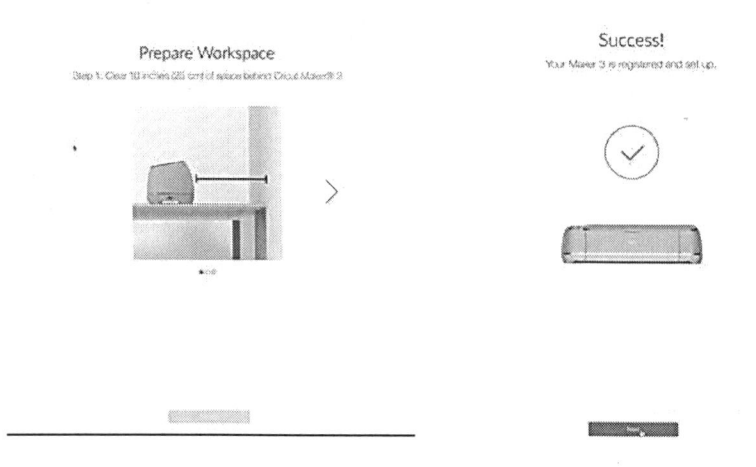

You do not need to subscribe to Cricut Access to start enjoying your dear Cricut Maker 3, it comes with an additional 100 ready-to-make projects. However, since all new machines come with a free trial of Cricut Access for a period of a month, it is recommended that you take advantage of it to enjoy thousands of fonts, images, and project designs. If you are a craft professional or you are currently embarking on a craft project and exhibitions, it is recommended you subscribe to either monthly or annual membership. Don't forget that Premium membership is only available on yearly subscription only, while the Standard membership of Cricut Access can be either monthly or yearly.

Making Your First Cut

Your newly unboxed machine comes with 4 sample Smart Materials to practice with. Ideally, after setting up your machine, the next thing to do is to perform a test. Follow the steps below to guide you through your first cut:

Step 1: In the Design Space, select your desired image.

Step 2: Slot in your desired Smart Material from the ones provided. Ensure the Smart Material is underneath the white guides.

Step 3: On the left side of your machine, locate the **Load** arrow and press it in order to load in your Smart Material very well.

Your machine will straighten out the material and measure it as well to ensure that you have enough for the design cut.

Step 4: Ensure that your Fine-Point Blade is secure in the clamp labelled **B**.

Step 5: Afterwards, click the **Start** button to start cutting your Smart material.

Step 6: Wait for the cutting to complete, and then press the **Unload** button on the machine.

Using Bluetooth in Cricut Maker 3

Bluetooth wireless connectivity makes the whole Cricut machines' setup a very tidy outlook. Although you can also make use of the USB cable, the machine has a docking space on top of it where you can place your smartphone or tablet. It still looks tidy, regardless.

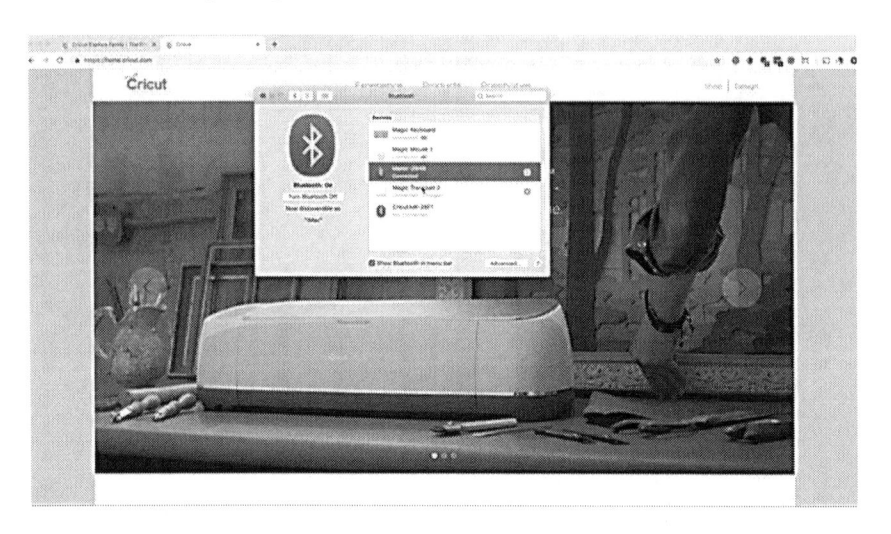

Follow these steps below to connect to Cricut Maker 3 using Bluetooth:

Step 1: Turn on Bluetooth on your smartphone or tablet or your PC. Ensure your device or PC is not more 3-4 meters away from your Cricut Maker 3 machine.

Step 2: Turn on your Cricut Maker 3 machine by putting on the power outlet and pressing the **Power** button on your machine.

Step 3: On your device or PC, click **Add Bluetooth or other device** or just let it search for nearby devices.

Step 4: Wait patiently for the device or PC to recognize and show the Cricut Maker 3 in the list. Then click on it to select.

Step 5: That's it. Your Cricut Maker 3 is now connected with your PC or device.

Pairing the Machine with a Computer

If during the setting up of your Cricut Maker 3 with your PC, a screen appears showing Connect to Computer via Bluetooth, it is because Design Space software has detected an AMD Ryzen chip on your PC. Some Windows AMD Ryzen chips have issues with USB connectivity. It is recommended that only Bluetooth connection be used for such PCs with Design Space software. However, Cricut recommends the USB hub with your PC if you still wish to use USB as your main connection:

> j5create 7-port USB 3.0 Hub

The previous section only shows how to connect via Bluetooth for a one-off project job. It will require a repeated process where each other there is need to connect to the machine to perform a task. To permanently have a connection that recognises the PC each time by itself, you will need to pair your Cricut Maker 3 with the PC. You won't need to search and set it up each time after following the steps below to pair your Cricut Maker 3 to your PC.

To pair, follow the steps below:

Step 1: Press the **Power** button on your Cricut Maker 3. If you are using the older models of Explore (Cricut

Explore or Cricut Explore One) then insert your Wireless Bluetooth Adapter to it. Make sure your Cricut machine is not too far from the PC. Let it not be more than 10-12 feet away.

Step 2: Check if your PC is Bluetooth enabled. If you are not sure your PC is Bluetooth enabled, go to the **Start** button on your PC's display screen and right-click on it. Then click **Device Manager**. If Bluetooth is there, then your PC is Bluetooth enabled.

Nevertheless, if it is not there, you will need to get a Bluetooth dongle to make your PC be able to connect with other Bluetooth devices. If you are buying a Bluetooth dongle, it is recommended you buy the ones that support audio devices. This is because not all Bluetooth dongles work well with Cricut machines, but those, which support audio devices, have reportedly been successful. Cricut out rightly advises that Cambridge Silicon Radio Bluetooth Dongles do not work with Cricut machines.

Close **Device Manager** when done.

Step 3: Click on the **Start** menu and open **Settings**. Alternatively, you can use the keyboard combination by pressing the **Windows key + I key** to open **Settings**.

Step 4: Locate **Devices** from the list of options and click it.

Step 5: Turn on the Bluetooth and click **Add Bluetooth or other device**.

Step 6: Click **Bluetooth** and wait patiently for your Cricut machine to be recognized and shown in the list.

Step 7a: Click the Cricut machine's name shown to connect.

Step 7b: If it asks for a PIN, then type **0000** and click **Connect**.

Your PC is now paired with your Cricut machine.

Resetting the Cricut Maker 3

To hard reset your Cricut Maker 3, do the following:

Step 1: Turn off the Cricut machine

Step 2: Then hold down the following 3 buttons – the power button, upload and unload buttons at the same time. Do not release until you see a rainbow screen.

Step 3: follow the prompts to calibrate the screen and finish up the hard reset.

However, if you are having an issue with your Design Space, you can also reset it. To do this, follow the steps below:

Step 1: Locate the **LocalData** folder and select all the files there. To be sure of selecting all that is in there;

use the keyboard combination by pressing **Ctrl key + A key.**

Step 2: Afterwards, use the keyboard combination **Shift + Delete** keys to permanently remove everything in that folder.

Step 3: Now, open **Design Space** for Desktop.

Step 4: From the **System** menu, click **Force Reload**

This should resolve the issue and reset Design Space.

Finding the Current Version of Cricut Design Space

For optimal experience, it is recommended to use the latest version of Design Space. Every version of Design Space has a number to it and this number changes as you update from time to time. For each of the available operating systems, we shall go through the steps of the process of finding the latest version of Cricut Design Space.

Finding the Current Version of Cricut Design Space for Windows

To find the current version of Cricut Design Space on yours Windows PC, follow the steps below:

Step 1: Click on the triangular shaped **arrow** on the taskbar on your PC. Hidden icons will display.

Step 2: Move your mouse cursor on the Cricut Design Space icon

Step 3: The plugin version will show. That's what you are looking for.

Finding the Current Version of Cricut Design Space for Android

To find the current version of Cricut Design Space on yours Android device, follow the steps below:

Step 1: Launch the Cricut Design Space app.

Step 2: Sign in to Design Space.

Step 3: At the top-left of your screen, click the person-shaped icon to open the menu of the app.

Step 4: When the menu appears, the current version's number will be at the very bottom of the list.

Finding the Current Version of Cricut Design Space for iOS

To find the current version of Cricut Design Space on yours iOs devices, follow the steps below:

Step 1: Launch the Cricut Design Space app.

Step 2: In the top-left of the screen where either your initials or profile picture are, click to open the app menu.

Step 3: When the menu appears, the current version number of the Design Space will be listed at the very bottom of the list.

Finding the Current Version of Cricut Design Space for Mac

To find the current version of Cricut Design Space on yours Mac, follow the steps below:

Step 1: In the top-right corner of your screen, click the Cricut icon

Step 2: Then select **About.**

Step 3: You will see the current version number of the Design Space in a small window that will appear.

Choosing Material Settings

As earlier noted, the Cricut Maker 3 can cut more than 300 types of materials. The Design space app has been programmed in the settings with a vast list of a variety of materials. This makes things so easy and faster, especially for beginners. However, you can select from the list of these settings and create your own.

To choose a material settings for your project, depending on your Operating System or device, follow the steps in the following sub-sections on how to create, edit and delete custom material settings.

Using a Custom Material Setting in Windows or Mac

To use a custom material setting in Windows or Mac, follow the steps below:

Step 1: On your Windows PC or Mac computer, launch the Design Space application and sign in.

Step 2: Then open a project, or create a project.

Step 3: Put on your Cricut Maker 3 machine

Step 4: Connect your Cricut Maker 3 to your Windows PC or Mac computer via Bluetooth or USB cable.

Step 5: Then on your computer, go on to the **Project Preview** screen.

Step 6: Then select **Browse All Materials**

Step 7: You can either **search** for a material or use the **All Categories** dropdown to make it faster to get to the material of your choice. Otherwise, you will have to scroll through the list there. Note that Cricut Smart Materials are the ones with the Cricut logo beside them.

Using a Custom Material Setting in Android or iOS

To use a custom material setting in Android or iOS, follow the steps below:

Step 1: On your device, launch the Design Space app and sign in.

Step 2: Then open a project, or create a project.

Step 3: Put on your Cricut Maker 3 machine.

Step 4: Connect your Cricut Maker 3 to your Android or iOS device through Bluetooth.

Step 5: Then on your device, go on to the Project Preview screen.

Step 6: Then select **All Materials** on the Set Material screen.

Step 7: You can either **search** for a material to make it faster to get to the material of your choice. Otherwise, you will have to scroll through the list there. Note that Cricut Smart materials are the ones with the Cricut logo beside them.

Custom Cut Settings of the Cricut Machine

To set a custom cut of your Cricut machine, follow the steps below:

Step 1: Open the Design Space app

Step 2: Click the 3 horizontal lines ☰ to open app menu.

Step 3: Click **Manage custom materials** from the dropdown menu

Step 4: On the top left, select **Cricut device.**

Step 5: Ensure to put the Cricut Maker 3 machine on.

Step 6: Connect your Cricut machine to your device or computer through Bluetooth.

Step 7: A vast list of all sorts of materials will appear. Beside each material, there is a value for the **Cut Pressure**, which is already set. If you wish to add your own, click on the **Cut Pressure figure** and shift the **Slider value bar** until you have reached a satisfactory number. Alternatively, simply make use of the **+/-** buttons.

Step 8: Then beside Cut Pressure is **Multi-cut**. Every material has **Cut pressure** and **Multi-cut** beside them. When you click on the **Multicut** options, you will choose between **select off, 2x, 3x, 4x...etc**, depending on the material.

Multi-cut setting is for directing your Cricut machine to cut for as many times as you have selected over the same design. For thicker materials, the higher the number of cuts, the better.

Step 9: You can also change the **blade type.** Here you select between **regular** or **deep cut**.

Step 10: Afterwards, when you are satisfied with your settings, click **save** beside **cancel** on each of the settings of each material. Use the **cancel** to reverse changes.

Please note that you add new material if it is not there. Also when you are done with the cut setting and it is saved, it will be stored and attached to your user ID. In other words, it will remember it and make it available to you each time you want to use it.

How to Create a New Custom Material

You can create your own custom materials list if the material you are looking for or a material setting is not in the pre-programmed lists. It is actually simple to do this. Note that creating new custom materials settings on the Design Space app for Android is presently not possible. But any new custom materials added from the other operating systems – Windows, Mac, iOS – will be available on Android. For now, you cannot add.

To create new custom material settings, follow the steps below:

Step 1: Open the Design Space app,

Step 2: Click the 3 horizontal lines ☰ to open app menu.

Step 3: Click **Manage custom materials** from the dropdown menu or click **Material Settings** at the bottom of the page.

Step 4: Locate and click **Add New Material** at the bottom of the list.

Step 5: Name the material and click **save**. That's all.

Step 6: You can now do a **cutting setting** on the new material by:

- adjusting the **Cut Pressure** by moving the slider bar or by using the **+/-** buttons
- selecting the preferred **Multi-cut** (recommended for thicker materials)
- Selecting the **Blade Type.**

Step 7: When you are done, ensure to click **save** to apply changes.

Step 8: Finally close the screen by clicking on the **X** at the upper right of the screen.

Your newly added material is now saved and you can easily search for it whenever you want to use the settings for your projects. In case, you are going to be using the newly added regularly, you can add it to your favorites by clicking the star symbol. Next time you need to work with it, you will easily find it in your favourites.

Installing the Bluetooth Adapter to the Cricut Machine

When using Cricut Maker 3 or Cricut Explore 3, you do not need a Bluetooth Wireless Adapter, because Bluetooth is in-built in them. Cricut Maker, Cricut Explore Air, and Cricut Explore Air 2 do not also need an adapter, because they also have in-built Bluetooth.

However, for the older models of the Explore series, the Explore and Explore One machines, you will need to use a Bluetooth adapter.

To install the Bluetooth adapter in the Explore or Explore One machines, follow the steps below:

Step 1: Connect the cutting machine to the power outlet and press the power button to turn it on.

Step 2: The adapter has a cap - remove it and insert into the Cricut Explore machine. When the tip of the adapter glows with blue light, you can push it any further.

Step 3: With the Bluetooth adapter now in place, the Cricut Explore or Cricut Explore One can now be set up to connect either with your device or computer as guided in Sections 3.2 and 3.3.

It is important that you remove the Bluetooth adapter when you are packing the machine, or moving it from place to place, because of possible damage. The adapter sticks out, and so it can easily be damaged and can also damage the USB port.

CHAPTER FOUR

Tools and Accessories Needed to Work with Cricut Maker 3

There are several tools and accessories the Cricut Maker 3 uses, but the Cricut Roll Holder and the rotary blade are unique to it. While you can use other tools and accessories in the Explore series too, you cannot use the roll holder and the rotary blade with them.

There are basically 3 classifications of the tools and accessories needed to work with the Cricut Maker 3 cutting machine. They are:

1. Machine tools
2. Cutting Mats
3. Craft tools

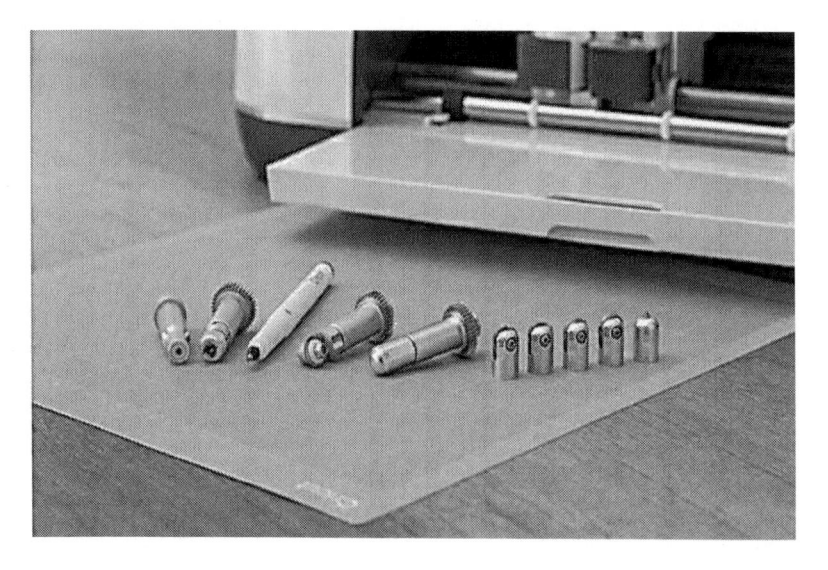

In a broader sense, however, we shall be discussing the different types of tools, one by one in no particular order.

1. **The Rotary Blade.** This is an awesome and powerful tool that is unique to Cricut Maker 3. It is used to cut a lot of fabrics, felt and quilt, without a stabilizer on the back to support it. It is better to have a replacement blade so that you are not stranded in the middle of a project, should anything happen to your main rotary blade after a long time of use.
2. **Knife Blade and Housing.** To cut thicker materials like chipboard, bass wood, or leather, you must have a knife blade. They usually last long.
3. **QuickSwap Housing and Tips Bundles**. This is a must have bundle with various tools that will make you really appreciate being a proud owner of this incredible amazing cutting machine. You can effortlessly swap with any of the QuickSwap tips you want to work with your Cricut Maker 3, by pressing a button. There is only one QuickSwap housing you need, which will work with all Cricut tips.
Let's quickly review the 6 tips.
    - **Engraving Tip** – engrave designs on paper, acrylic, wood and other materials.
    - **Debossing Tip** – to create images on materials.
    - **Perforation blade** – to perforate materials like raffle tickets that can be torn off.
    - **Scoring Wheel** – for scoring crisp lines in materials

- **Double Scoring Wheel** – scores two parallel lines, good for scoring craft board, cardboard and other heavier materials.
- **Wavy Blade** – It is a rotary blade used for making wavy edges on your decorations of flowers, cards, fabrics etc.

4. **Mats** – The Cricut cutting mats are sticky so as to make materials stay in place to make precise and neat cutting. However, with time, the stickiness fades away and you will need to replace them.
FabricGrip mat, strong grip mat, LightGrip and StandardGrip are the types of mat available.

LightGrip mat: this is the best mat for cutting copy paper, thin cardstock, normal vinyl, and so on, because of its light grip. It is blue in color.

StandardGrip mat: this is best used for medium-weight materials such as glitter cardstock, glitter iron-ons, corrugated cardboards and so on. It is green in color.

StrongGrip mat: This is best used for heavier materials such as balsa wood, poster board, leather, chipboard and so on, because of its strong grip. It is purple in color.

FabricGrip mat: This is specifically designed for fabric. It needs cleaning often as it gets dirty quickly. It is pink in color.

5. **Cricut Markers and Pens** – are used to write and draw. The Clamp labelled **A** holds the pens. You can use your Design Space app to look for a good writing font that will give you a beautiful handwriting job. There are numerous fonts in the app free of charge. Cricut Infusible Ink Markers are great tools to draw custom designs.

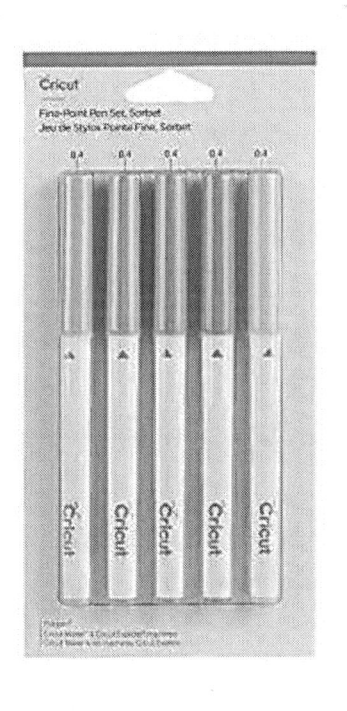

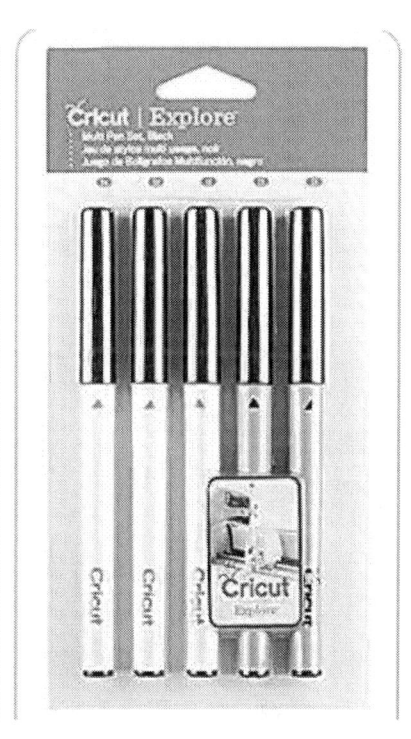

6. **Cricut Fabric Pen** – used to mark out your pattern on fabric for sewing projects.

7. **Foil Transfer Kit** – this is another accessory specifically made to work with your Cricut Maker. Beautiful foil accents can be added to your projects with this kit.

The Foil Transfer Kit has the following:

- 1 Foil Transfer Tool Housing.
- 3 Foil Transfer Tips – fine, medium, bold.
- 12 Foil Transfer Sheets 4" x 6" (10.1 cm x 15.2 cm) 4 each of Gold, Silver and White.
- And a tape.

8. **Brayer and Removal tools** – smoothen out fabric, cardstock or vinyl on the mat so that there are no wrinkles. The tweezers are used to remove tiny fabrics or other materials stuck to the mat.
9. **Basic Tool Kit** – used to remove paper and cardstock from the mats. The kit includes a spatula, burnisher, weeder, tweezers, a pair of scissors with a cover.

10. **XL Scrapper** – is a bigger scrapper and will weed vinyl off the mats quite faster and conveniently.

11. **Cricut Sewing Kit** includes tools for sewing and quilting. The tools are a tape measure, a leather thimble, fabric shears, pins, seam ripper, thread snips, and pin cushion.

12. **Cricut Machine Tote** –this is a bag to put your Cricut cutting machine if you need to travel or you just want to keep it away.

13. **Rolling Craft Tote** – is used for keeping all your accessories and materials for the move.

14. **EasyPress 2** – is used for transferring your iron-on vinyl design projects. It comes in 4 sizes. The Easy Press 2 is best used with Cricut Infusible ink.

15. **BrightPad** – is also used in weeding vinyl.

16. **Fabulous Storage Cart** – it is a storage cart with drawers to put your Cricut Maker and accessories as well.

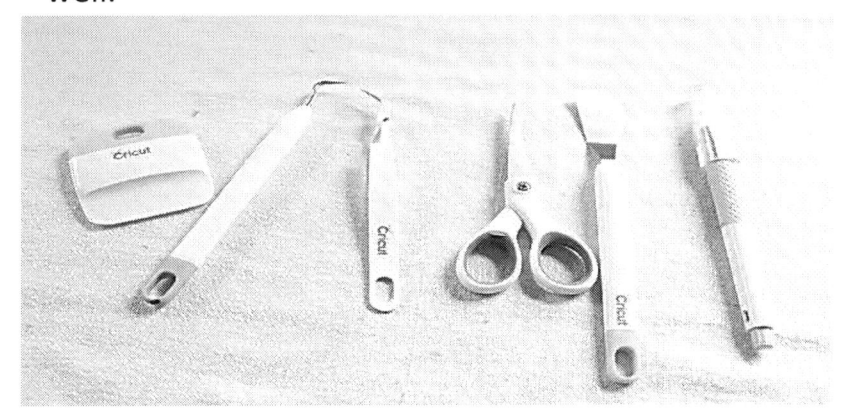

Materials

It is amazing that the Cricut Maker 3 can cut a wide range of materials from vinyls, fabrics, woods, papers, stickers, iron-on vinyls, leathers and more. So, if you are dreaming of making decorations and organizing projects, the Cricut Maker 3 is just the perfect dream maker. There are some materials Cricut Machine can cut that you can infuse into your projects.

What materials does the Cricut Maker 3 cut? The Cricut Maker 3 can cut most materials less than 2.4mm thick. It cuts better with precision than scissors or an x-acto knife could ever do. It can cut more than 300 types of materials. Find below a long list of some materials your Cricut Maker 3 can do.

1. Copy paper
2. Notebook paper
3. Flat cardboard
4. Cereal box
5. Adhesive cardstock
6. Cardstock
7. Glitter paper
8. Glitter cardstock
9. Construction paper
10. Post-its
11. Photographs
12. Photoframing mat
13. Scrapbook paper
14. Poster board
15. Metallic paper
16. Metallic poster board
17. Metallic cardstock
18. Freezer paper
19. Paper board
20. Paper foil
21. Watercolor paper
22. Solid core cardstock
23. Rice paper
24. Embossed foil
25. Paper grocery bag
26. Pearl paper
27. Pearl cardstock
28. Wax paper
29. Kraft board
30. Kraft paper
31. Kraft board foil
32. Shimmer paper
33. White core cardstock
34. Parchment paper
35. Smart paper sticker cardstock
36. 2mm chipboard
37. 1.5mm Kraft chipboard
38. Corrugated cardboard
39. Outdoor vinyl
40. Matte vinyl
41. Metallic vinyl
42. Pearl metallic vinyl
43. Dry Erase vinyl
44. Glossy vinyl
45. Glitter vinyl
46. Shimmer vinyl
47. True brushed vinyl
48. Chalkboard vinyl
49. Smart Vinyl, Shimmer
50. Smart vinyl, permanent
51. Smart vinyl, matte metallic
52. Smart vinyl, removable
53. Adhesive vinyl
54. Permanent vinyl
55. Removable vinyl
56. Holographic crystals vinyl
57. Holographic sparkle vinyl
58. Stencil vinyl
59. Printable vinyl
60. Printable iron on
61. Everyday iron on
62. Iron on lite
63. Patterned iron on
64. Mosaic iron on

65. Foil iron on
66. Flocked iron on
67. Glitter iron on
68. Matte iron on
69. Holographic sparkle iron on
70. Neon iron on
71. Express iron on
72. Sport Flex iron on
73. Glossy iron on
74. Smart iron on
75. Smart iron on, glitter
76. Smart iron on, holographic
77. Mesh iron on
78. Metallic iron on
79. Denim
80. Burlap
81. Fleece
82. Polyester
83. Tulle
84. Linen
85. Canvas
86. Duck cloth
87. Jersey
88. Metallic leather
89. Leather
90. Tweed
91. Silk
92. Cotton fabric
93. Jute
94. Seersucker
95. Terry cloth
96. Felt
97. Wood felt
98. Chiffon
99. Flannel
100. Muslin
101. Soft metallic leather
102. Cashmere
103. Knits
104. Velvet
105. Faux suede
106. Faux leather
107. Moleskin
108. Printable fabric
109. Oil cloth
110. Adhesive foil
111. Balsa wood
112. Duct tape
113. Paint chips
114. Soda can
115. Washi tape
116. Washi sheets
117. Foil acetate
118. Adhesive wood
119. Shrink plastic
120. Cork board
121. Plastic packaging
122. Birch wood
123. Basswood
124. Metallic vellum
125. Stencil material
126. Aluminium sheets
127. Aluminium foil
128. Transparency film
129. Craft foam
130. Vellum
131. Printable sticker paper
132. Printable magnet sheets
133. Magnet sheets
134. Corrugated paper
135. Wrapping paper
136. Embossable foil
137. Tissue paper
138. Glitter foam
139. Wood veneer
140. Temporary tattoo paper
141. Window cl

Installing a Pen

The Cricut machine has two clamps labelled **A** and **B**. The Clamp labelled **A** is used with pens. You will need to change pens from time to time as there are different types of pens. Follow these simple steps to install a pen:

Step 1: Open the clamp labelled **A**.

Step 2: Insert the pen you desire to install.

Step 3: Use a little firm and gentle force until it clicks.

Step 4: You are done; close the clamp.

Note that for the old model, Cricut Explore One, a Cricut Pen Adapter is required in order to install any pen.

Selecting Pens

The Cricut cutting machines are primarily cutting machines, and the Cricut Design Space is also set to cut. Nevertheless, Cricut machines also write and draw. This is the reason you have two clamps labelled **A** and **B**. The clamp labelled **A** is for holding pens and markers. You will therefore need to tell your Cricut machine that you want it to use pens. To do this, follow the steps below:

Step 1: Launch your Design Space and go to the canvas area

Step 2: At the top right corner, select either **Maker**, **Explore** or **Joy**, being the model name of your Cricut machine.

Step 3: Afterwards, select the layer, either text or image you want to work with

Step 4: Then change the **Operation** to **Pen**.

Step 5a: You can change the color and the type of pen you wish to use when you select **draw**. If you don't, the default setting is to use Black Fine Point pen. To change it, you will find a small color box beside **Operation** – click it and select your desired color and type of pen.

Step 5b: In case you are using more than a color, it is advisable you set the type of pen and color and assign them accordingly in the desired order. Otherwise, the machine will use random order to color and use the wrong pen.

You may need to note that not all pens are in the database. So when selecting your pen color, ensure to match the size and color of the pen as nearly accurate as possible. For instance, when you select a Calligraphy pen, the silver pen won't appear. You can still use a silver calligraphy pen, but you will have to select a silver color from a different size.

Cricut Pen and Markers Products

The following are Cricut pens and markers products:

1. Extra fine point pen set
2. Infusible ink markers 1.0
3. Glitter gel pen set
4. Multi pen set

5. Ultimate fine point pen set
6. Metallic pen set
7. Antiquity pen set
8. Washable fabric pen
9. Extra fine point pen set
10. Cricut Joy infusible ink
11. Ultimate extra fine point set
12. Ultimate gel pen set
13. Milky gel pen set

Types of Cricut Pens

All Cricut pens are permanent when they dry up, except the Glitter gel pen. Cricut pens are to be used on paper and non-coated materials, but not on glitter cardstock, vinyl and other coated and glossy materials.

Cricut pens can be in ink, gel, glitter, metallic, and so on. They are also in various colors.

Cricut pens are sold in packages or even in boxes. A box usually contains 30 pens. Each pen has a label and name that will help you to quickly know the type and the size.

Basically, there are different categories of Cricut pens. In each category, there are numerous options of colors to select from.

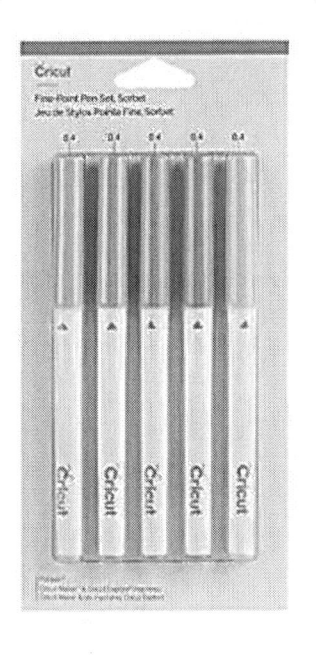

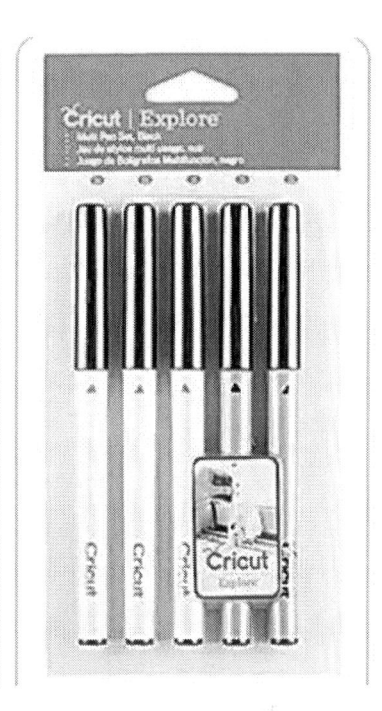

Types of Cricut Pens (used on any series except Cricut Joy)

These are types of Cricut pens you should be familiarized with:

1. **Extra Fine (XF) – 0.3 mm**
   The pen is transparent and has **XF** written at the bottom of the pen. Not many colors are available for this type of pen.
2. **Fine (F) – 0.4 mm**
   The pen is white and has **F** written at the bottom of the pen. There are many colors available for this type and size of pen. They are the most common and are used for coloring decorations, invitations, cards and tags.

The Cricut Infusible Ink pens are Fine pens and also 0.4 mm size. They are used for transferring to polyester-coated materials (such as totes, t-shirts, and so on) with the aid of your EasyPress.

3. **Glitter Gel (GG) – 0.8 mm**

    The pen is opaque with a glitter cap and has **GG** written at the bottom of the pen. This type of pen adds extra glittering details to your projects.

4. Gel (g) – 1mm

    The pen is white and has **G** written at the bottom of the pen. It adds a smooth and silky look to your project.

5. **Marker (M) – 1 mm**

    The pen is white and has **M** written at the bottom of the pen. They are mainly in black, silver, gold and other metallic colors. The Fabric Pen and the Cricut Infusible Ink Markers are also of this pen size and work just as the Infusible Ink Pens.

6. **Calligraphy (C) – 2.0/2.5 mm**

    They are quite different from other pens and markers. They are usually white in color and have C written at the bottom. The body of the Black Calligraphy Pen is grey though. They are available in black and other metallic colors such as gold and silver. They are used for calligraphy of handwritten fonts.

    When installing your calligraphy pen, ensure it is tilted to 45°. Every pen has an arrow mark, which shows the direction to insert. Note and follow this arrow mark when installing a calligraphy pen on your Cricut machine.

Types of Cricut Pens used with Cricut Joy

It is noteworthy to mention here that some pens are specifically meant for the Cricut Joy machine, because of its portable size. This will make you not to mistakenly purchase the wrong pens. Because of the Cricut Joy machine's size, the clamp is smaller, so the pens are also smaller. There is no calligraphy pen for use in the Cricut Joy machine. Projects on the Cricut Joy are also smaller.

The steps for installing pens instructed previously will work here too. Same as the steps for selecting a pen on the Design Space app or software instructed in previously will work just the same.

The following are the types of pens and markers used with the Cricut Joy machine:

- Fine Pen 0.4
- Extra Fine Pen 0.3
- Marker 1.0 mm
- Glitter Gel Pen 0.8 mm
- Gel Pen 1.0 mm
- Infusible Ink Pen 0.4 mm
- Infusible Ink Marker 1.0 mm
- Marker 1.0 mm

Specific Blades and Tools for Cricut Maker 3

The following are specific blades and tools for Cricut Maker 3:

1. Cricut roll holder
2. Foil transfer tool replacement tips
3. QuickSwap housing
4. Rotary blade and drive housing
5. Engraving tip and quickswap housing
6. Debossing tip
7. Perforation blade
8. Wavy blade and quickswap housing
9. Scoring wheel tip and drive housing
10. Knife blade replacement kit
11. Foil transfer kit
12. Bonded-fabric replacement blade and housing
13. Deep-point blade and housing
14. Premium fine point replacement blades

How to Tell your Cricut Machine to Write and Draw

The Cricut Design Space is primarily set to cut. However, Cricut machines also write and draw. This is the reason you have two clamps labelled A and B. The clamp labelled A is for holding pens and markers. You will therefore need to tell your Cricut machine that you want it to use pens. To do this, follow the steps below:

Step 1: Launch your Design Space and go to the canvas area

Step 2: At the top right corner, select from either - **Maker**, **Explore** or **Joy**, being the model name of your Cricut machine.

Step 3: Afterwards, select the layer, either text or image you want to work with

Step 4: Then change the **Operation** to **Pen**.

Step 5a: You can change the color and the type of pen you wish to use when you select **draw**. If you don't, the default setting is to use Black Fine Point pen. To change it, you will find a small color box beside **Operation** – click it and select your desired color and type of pen.

Step 5b: In case you are using more than a color, it is advisable you set the type of pen and color and assign them accordingly in the desired order. Otherwise, the machine will use random order to color and use the wrong pen.

You may need to note that not all pens are in the database. So when selecting your pen color, ensure to match the size and color of the pen as nearly accurate as possible. For instance, when you select a Calligraphy pen, the silver pen won't appear. You can still use a silver calligraphy pen, but you will have to select a silver color from a different size.

CHAPTER FIVE

Different Blades for Different Materials

As earlier discussed in the previous chapter, blades are major tools in your Cricut machine as they are used for cutting. There are different types of blades, because there are different types of materials, which also have varied thickness and texture.

The Cricut Maker 3 can cut most materials less than 2.4mm thick. It cuts smoothly with precision than scissors or an x-acto knife could ever do. It can cut more than 300 types of materials.

1. **Fine Point Blade and Premium Fine Point Blade.** They are used for cutting intricate designs on a long list of various thin and medium weight materials. It will work well on cardstock, poster board, vinyl, office paper, iron-on and so on. It has a 45-degree angle. It is the pre-installed blade that comes with your Cricut machine.
2. **Deep Point Blade** is used to cut thicker materials. It cuts materials such as chipboard, magnet paper, cardboard and so on. This blade is made of harder and stronger steel compared with the Fine Point Blade. It has a 60-degree angle.
3. **Bonded Fabric Blade** cuts bonded fabric. It is best used with the Fabric Grip mat, because the mat stabilizes the grip on the material.

4. **The Rotary Blade.** This awesome and powerful tool is unique to Cricut Maker 3. It is used to cut a lot of fabrics, felt and quilt, without a stabilizer on the back to support it.
5. **Knife Blade and Housing.** To cut thicker materials like chipboard, bass wood, balsa wood or leather, you must have a knife blade. They usually last long.
6. **Deep Cut Blade, Standard Blade, Cake Blade, Scoring Blade.** These blades are used with older models. They cannot be used with the Cricut Maker 3, or any of the Maker series. To distinguish them from blades used in newer models, they are shaped differently with different colors.
7. **QuickSwap Housing and Tips Bundles.** This is a must have bundle with various tools that will make you really appreciate being a proud owner of this incredible amazing cutting machine. You can effortlessly swap with any of the QuickSwap tips you want to work with your Cricut Maker 3, by pressing a button. There is only one QuickSwap housing you need, which will work with all Cricut tips.

Let's quickly review the 6 tips.
- **Engraving Tip** – engrave designs on paper, acrylic, wood and other materials.
- **Debossing Tip** – to create images on materials.
- **Perforation blade** – to perforate materials such as raffle tickets that can be torn off.
- **Scoring Wheel** – for scoring crisp lines in materials

- **Double Scoring Wheel** – scores two parallel lines, good for scoring craftboard, cardboard and other heavier materials.
- **Wavy Blade** – It is a rotary blade used to make wavy edges on your decorations of flowers, cards, fabrics etc.

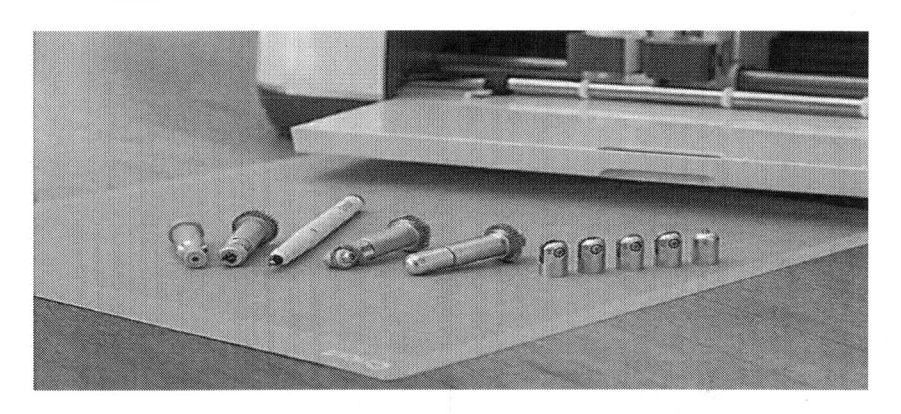

How to Calibrate the Cricut Knife Blade

When using your Cricut Knife Blade for the very first time, you should ensure to calibrate it. This is to test if it is working properly. To calibrate your Cricut Knife Blade, follow the steps below:

Step 1: Open the Design Space app

Step 2: Go to **Account** menu

Step 3: Click **Calibration**

Step 4: Then select **Knife Blade**

Step 5: Then insert the Knife Blade into the Clamp labelled **B** in your machine.

Step 6: Place a white paper on the mat.

Step 7: Go back to the Design Space app, and click **Continue**.

Step 8: On your Cricut machine, press the **Go** button.

Step 9: When done, take the mat out of the machine

Step 10: Check the paper for the set of lines the machine has cut. There should be 7 sets. Some lines overlap or almost overlap themselves. The set of lines that is best overlapped and appears almost like a single is what you are looking for. Count from 1 to know which one it is.

Step 11: On your Design Space app, put the number in the prompt that appears there. That is it, it is calibrated.

Changing the Blades of the Cricut Machine

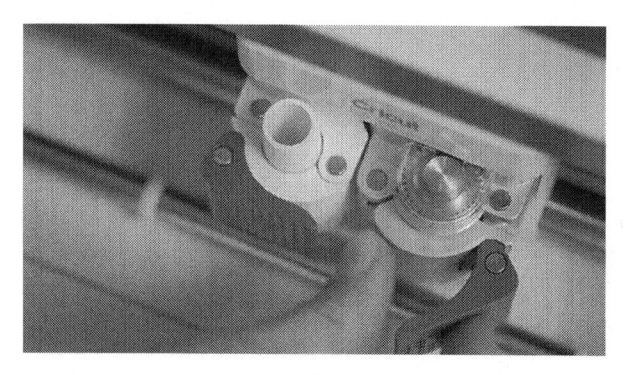

You will need to know how to change the blades, because you cannot use this same blade all the time. Due to the fact that you will be working with different materials, sometimes in a singular project, you will be changing the blade from time to time.

More so, your Cricut blades will need replacement at some point. Another reason why you should know how to change your machine's blade is so that you can bring it out to sharpen after a while.

Blade housings used in the Cricut Maker 3 cannot be used in the other models, though most blades can. And so, there will be slight differences in the way the blades are changed in each model. While this guide is primarily focussing on the Cricut Maker 3, it will sometimes include what is obtainable in other models.

To change the blade of your Cricut machine, please follow these steps below:

Step 1: The first thing to do is to remove the blade housing from your Cricut Maker 3 machine by opening the Clamp labelled **B** on the double tool holder. Remember that the Clamp labelled **A** is primarily for pens.

But for older models of Cricut machines, you will only have to unscrew the black arm holding the blade housing. Then remove it.

Step 2: Here you will remove the blade from the housing. It is very important that you put something under the housing you are holding, so that when you eject the blade from the housing, the blade won't fall off and get missing. You can position a mat or tray right under your housing held in your hand.

Step 2a: For **Fine Point Blade housing, Premium Fine Point Blade housing, Deep Point Blade housing and Deep Cut Blade housing,** locate a pin on top of the housing and press it. Then remove the blade from the bottom.

Step 2b: For Knife Blade housing, place the changing lid (that comes with your purchase of a replacement) over the blade and the housing sleeve. Then hold the housing very well in one hand and twist the changing cap anti-clockwise with the other hand. Turn around the housing and it will slide out.

Step 2c: For Rotary Blade housing, place the empty changing cap over the blade and housing sleeve and thereafter use the screwdriver to loosen the blade nut. Blades are sharp and can be injurious, that is the reason for the changing cap.

Step 3: It is time to make your new blade. Simply remove the protective plastic cover from the new replacement blade. If it is a Knife Blade or Rotary Blade you want to change to, it is their protective changing caps you remove. It is recommended you don't thrash them, because you can put old blades in them to protect from accidental cuts on users.

Step 4: The next thing is to insert the new blade into its appropriate housing. Again, we will look at the different types. However, it is important to note that blades must be put in the correct corresponding housings. Also, take cognizance of the model of your machine and be sure the housings are compatible.

Step 4a: Inserting Fine Point, Premium Fine Point, Deep Point and Deep Cut Blades into their housings. First, put your new blade into the correct housing meant for the blade. Then gently insert the blade into the hole at the bottom of the blade housing, so that only the tip is showing. There is a magnet inside that should ensure that the blade is in place anyway.

Step 4b: Inserting Knife Blade into its housing. Put your blade into the hole at the bottom of the suitable housing for it, ensuring that the indent is aligned with the groove inside the housing. Screw it and turn the changing cap very well to make it tight. Then remove and keep (or thrash) the changing cap.

Step 4c: Inserting Rotary Blade into its housing. Here, insert the new blade into the hole at the bottom of the housing. Then screw back the housing screw that holds the black arm.

Step 5: Finally install the blade housing back to the clamp labelled **B**, from where it was removed. Then close it by pushing down the Clamp B so that it aligns with Clamp **B**. That's all.

For older Cricut machines, put the blade housing right inside the black arm and screw it until it is tight.

How to Cut Lightweight and Heavyweight Materials

To cut materials with your Cricut Maker 3, just open up your Design Space app to select from the hundreds of images and designs and also set the material you want to use. The app will put through all you need. The material you want to cut will determine the kind of blade and mat (not necessary with Smart Materials) to use.

How to Cut Lightweight Materials

For lightweight materials, Fine Point Blade is the standard for Cricut Maker 3. The Knife Blade and the Rotary Blade are used for heavyweight materials.

Follow these steps below to cut on your machine:

Step 1: Put the pretty side of your material on the adhesive part of your mat.

Step 2: Be sure to install the appropriate blade in Clamp **B** of the machine

Step 3: Then open your Design Space app to choose a design. Ensure the material setting is as close to the material you are using as possible. Alternatively, you can do a custom setting.

Step 4a: If you are working on simple designs, just go to the **Make** screen and click **Fast Mode** to make it cut twice as fast. This should not be used on intricate cuts.

Step 4b: For intricate designs, go to **Browse All Materials**. Then locate the material with an intricate Cut written in front of it. For instance, **Cardstock – Intricate Cut**.

Step 5: When done, eject the mat and carefully remove your material from the mat.

How to Cut Heavyweight Materials

To cut heavyweight materials, you must ensure the appropriate blade must be installed in the Clamp labelled **B**. The Knife Blade is good to go, but it won't cut designs smaller than 3/4". Depending on the material and the design, a cut time varies. Fast mode won't be available when using the Knife Blade.

To cut heavyweight materials on your Cricut Maker 3, follow the steps below. Let's use wood.

Step 1: The Design Space app will tell you to move the star wheels to the extreme, because they can mar your material. So move it as the first step before any other thing. The available space for your material will then be 11" wide. If it is

12" wide, it will go over the wheel. Therefore, you will need to trim it to 11".

Step 2: Next put your material to your StrongGrip mat. You might also want to give it an additional grip by holding the edges down with a painter's tape. If you are using a Smart Material, you do not need a mat. You can use your Smart Material like that.

Step 3: Go to your Design Space app, and create a design. Before it is set, **Cut** and click **Make** It.

Step 4: Then select your material and be sure all settings are suitable and correct.

Step 6: Press **Go** on your Cricut machine. Depending on the complexity of your cut, wood will take close to an hour or more because it makes about 15 passes.

Step 7: When done, let out the mat.

Step 8: Then remove the tapes and gently remove the wood from the mat.

How to clean Your Cricut Maker 3 and the Necessary Materials to be used

Like any other machine, maintenance is very important, whether it is often used or not. The rate of maintenance, of course, depends on the rate of use. Since it is a cutting machine, there is doubt it will leave behind particles and debris that can affect the next task. It is important therefore that the machine, the cutting mat and other accessories are routinely cleaned. Some parts are greased and do not need to be cleaned.

When cleaning your cutting machine, be gentle and do not apply too much force. Do not clean or go near the gear chain right at the back of the blade housing compartment. Avoid using harsh chemicals such as acetone. Be sure that the wipes used are free of alcohol. Most importantly, your machine must be switched off. In fact, remove it totally from the power outlet.

Materials that should be used **for Cleaning** the Cricut maker

Cricut has cleaning kits in its online webstore, from which you can make orders. You can also decide to get them from anywhere else.

The following are cleaning materials that can be used in cleaning your Cricut machine:

1. Paper towels
2. Gentle cleaner
3. Microfiber cloths
4. Small brushes
5. Baby wipes
6. Canned air
7. Soap and water
8. Transfer tape

9. Scraper
10. Thick towel
11. Aluminium foil
12. And so on.

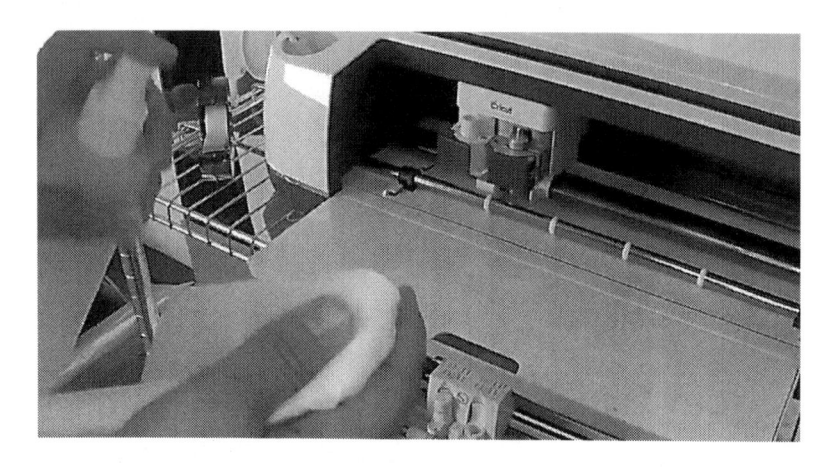

How to Clean the Cricut Maker

As earlier discussed, cleaning your machine is keeping your machine in good condition. It is important to note that the blades and the heat press should be kept in good condition all the time. It is as well important to keep the inside and the outside of your Cricut Maker machine clean. So, this guide will put you through on how to keep your mat, clamps, front rod, rear rod, heat press and blades of your Cricut Maker.

How to Clean the Front Rod in the Cricut Maker

Use a baby wipe to remove dust and debris on the front rod, but not the rear rod. The rear has lubricant spread across it and has a different method of cleaning.

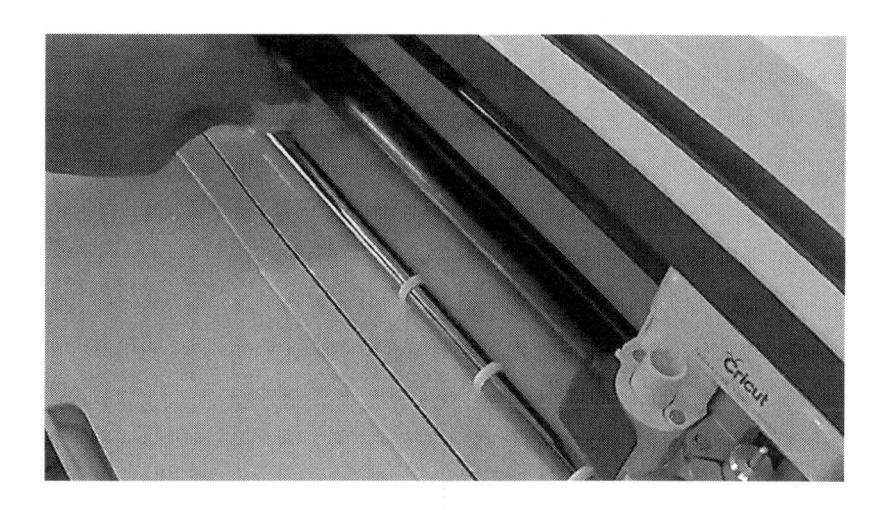

How to Clean the Cricut Blades in the Cricut Maker

The major reason the Cricut Blades must be kept clean is to reduce the rate at which they go dull. If dust and debris are left on them, they soon need to be replaced.

Remember, blades are sharp and are delicate to clean. They may end up cutting the cleaning material and creating more dirt. The best method of cleaning the fine point blade or deep point blade is to use an aluminium foil ball.

To do this, follow these steps below:

> **Step 1:** Detach the Blade and its attachment from the housing
>
> **Step 2:** press the button on the blade holder and stick it into your aluminium foil ball. Do this many times so that debris or pieces of vinyl may be removed.

Step 3: Remove the Blade tip and use a hard brush to clean off dust. Use the brush to clean the hole. Use canned air thereafter and finally use a paper towel to clean.

Step 4: Put back the blade tip and re-insert the blade attachment into the housing.

Step 5: Finally, put back the housing back into the clamp.

How to Clean the Cricut Heat Press in the Cricut Maker

Similar to the metal part of the pressing iron, the Cricut heat press plate is made of aluminium but coated with non-sticking ceramic.

What you are cleaning here is iron-on waste and sometimes dust particles. A liquid cleaner will clean the dust, but not the iron-on materials stuck on it.

To clean off the iron-on materials stuck on the plate while it is hot, a hard rag or thick towel can be used. However, if it is cool, you will need to heat it back up to about 350 degrees, and then clean. A clean heat press won't transfer anything when it is clean. You may want to do a small test on a piece of white cloth first, before you use it for a new and different project.

How to Clean the Mat in the Cricut Maker

Cricut cutting mats have an adhesive top layer for holding tight and steady the materials you are about to work with. After several times using it, the mat loses its grip, mainly because of dust and debris being stuck to it. You will need to replace them when this happens. However, if you can clean your mat, you will need to postpone replacing it until it can no longer stick.

You can clean your mats by using soap and water, tweezers, spatula, scraper, baby wipes, lint rollers or transfer tapes. But what you use depends on the kind of mat and what type of material you have just finished working with. Denim, for instance, leaves behind a lot of waste.

Follow this general steps to clean all types of mat, except the FabricGrip Mat:

> **Step 1:** Using a set of tweezers is the best way to remove larger chunks of debris. Scrapers may end up removing some of the adhesive surface. Baby wipes, soap and soap should not be used on FabricGrip mats.

> **Step 2:** After using the tweezers to remove larger debris, use a baby wipe to clean dust and light dirt. Ensure the baby wipe is non-bleaching and non-alcoholic. If they are, they will make the adhesive non-effective immediately.

Step 3: Finally, put your mat out to dry. If you use paper towel or cloth towel to dry the math, they will add more particles. After drying out the mat, it should stick as before.

To Clean the FabricGrip mat using the transfer tape, follow the steps below:

Step 1: Cut the transfer tape to fit the size of the mat.

Step 2: Put it on top of the mat, and press down. Use a scraper to smoothen it. The transfer tape is sticky too, so let it stick very well onto the mat.

Step 3: Afterwards, remove the transfer tape gently. The felt or fibers would have stuck to the transfer tape.

Step 4: That's it. Thrash the used transfer tape.

This is the best method to use to clean FabricGrip mats, and it is also a good method to use on any other mat. Remember not to use soap and water, baby wipes or scrapers on the FabricGrip mats.

Cleaning of the Clamps

Be careful when cleaning the Cricut Maker 3's Adaptive Tool System. There are two Clamps in the Cricut Maker 3 machine. For identification, they are labelled **A** and **B**. Clamp **A** is for pens and Clamp **B** is for the blades. To remember easily, take **A** as accessories and **B** for blades. These are vital features of the Cricut Maker 3 and you should maintain them and keep them in good condition at all times.

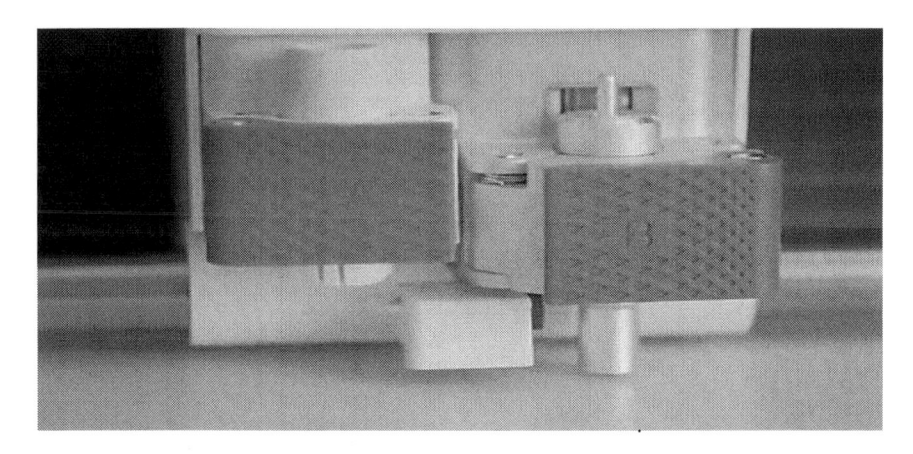

To clean them, simply use the canned air or a round brush to clean each of the clamps. It is always better to use canned air around delicate parts of the machine.

If you are using older makes of the Cricut machine, where a pen adapter has to be used; simply clean, the same way by using a round brush.

Cleaning the Rear Rod

The best thing is to leave the rod alone, as it usually has grease to make the machine function well. However, the grease collects debris sometimes and should be removed.

First, move your star wheels and use canned air to blow out debris from the rod. You can also use a brush to gently take away any debris. However, after the debris has been removed, use the brush to redistribute the grease along the rod again. In case, there is a grease stain on any other part of the machine, use your baby wipes to clean it off. When you are done, place the star wheels back and close your Cricut machine.

Cleaning the Outside of Your Cricut Machine

The body of the Cricut machine can also accumulate dust from external sources and also from debris during cuts. To clean the outside of your Cricut machine, follow the steps below:

Step 1: Apply a little of the cleaner on the body of your Cricut machine. Avoid using excess around the button area as too much liquid can leak inside and spoil it. It is best to spray the cleaner onto a paper towel and clean thoroughly to remove remarkable stains.

Step 2: Then use baby wipes for the rest of the body of your machine.

Step 3: Should there be excess cleaner, dry it off with a paper towel.

Step 4: Thereafter use a microfiber cloth to wipe the whole exterior for a thorough clean.

Step 5: Use the round brush for cleaning openings and crevices.

CHAPTER SIX

How to Design on Cricut Maker 3

Basically, the Design Space is the software used to design on the Cricut Maker 3. The Design Space is free of charge. It is available for Windows and Mac computer users and the mobile version is also available for use for phone and tablet users with the Android and iOS operating systems.

The Design Space has a library of ready-to-make projects with access to lots of free designs, images and fonts. You can also purchase others. The Design Space allows you to upload your own designs and images in the following acceptable formats - **.jpg, .gif, .png, .bmp, .dxf and .svg**.

The following steps should be taken to start a project:

Step 1: Open your Design Space app

Step 2: At the top left of the screen that opens, click New Project or the **+** symbol below it.

Step 3: A new blank canvas will appear. Be sure to select the right machine, if you have more than one machine.

Step 4: On the left of the screen is a menu panel that contains options together with their icons. They are:

New

Templates

Projects

Images

Text

Shapes

Upload

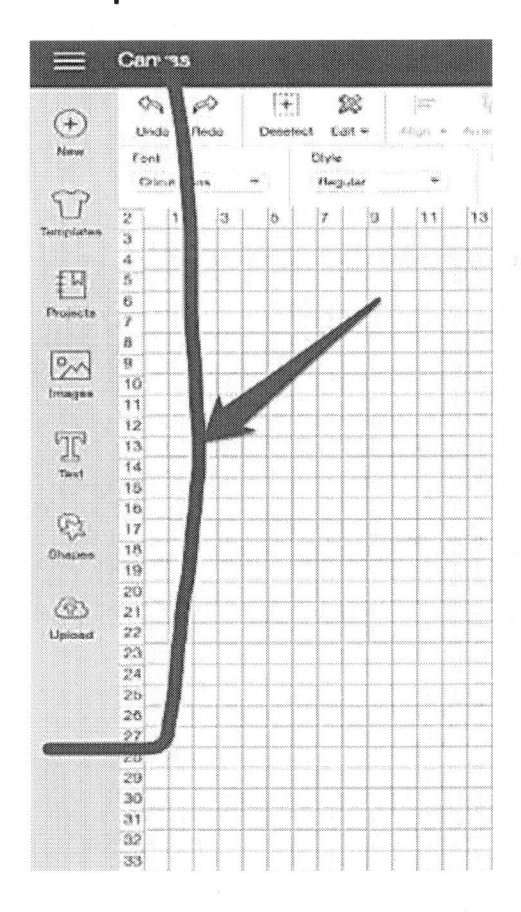

New. Click **New** if you want to start a new project. A blank screen will appear when you do. You will then be instructed to either save your current project or overwrite it with a new one you just opened. Here you have all the tools to help you create a new design.

Templates. Click here to have ready-made designs that you can modify to your taste. You can modify the size, space and type. This is like a short cut to that design you have in mind.

Projects. This is where to click to enter Cricut Access where all the ready-to-make designs are. The designs are ready, just select and make them. However, you can customize them to further suit what you have in mind. You can click on **Categories** to see a drop down menu of several options to select from. There are free ones, you will see them all grouped in a page if you select Free from the menu.

Images. When you are designing and you wish to insert an image on the canvas, click image. This will bring out thousands of images you can select from and to start working your design on. Because of the number of images, you can use the search bar to search for an image quickly. When searching, you can use Filters to further help you narrow down your search.

Then there is the **Linetype**, which has the following depending on the blade or pen inserted:

    Cut

    Draw

Score

Engrave

Deboss

Wave

Perf

Foil – Fine, Medium or Bold

You can also change the **Pen Type** by clicking on it. As you select the pen you wish to use, there will be changes in the image on the canvas.

If you intend to print your cut image, click **Fill**. A drop-down menu will appear, select **Print**. There is a little box beside **Fill** that when you click it, you can change the color of your image.

You can also change the pattern from the **Print Type** small window or click **Edit Pattern** at the bottom of that small window.

The size or scale of the image can be modified by sliding the slider either left or right in the **Edit Pattern** small window. The images can also be rotated here or flipped to either side.

The material color for a cut image can be changed. If two colors are chosen for two images, the machine will cut them in different mats. If you want to cut in the same mat, then ensure the material colors are the same.

Text. Click **Text** and you should be able to type in whatever you desire on the canvas. Texts can be edited from the options at the top left corner of the **Text** screen. **Font, Font Style, Font Size, Letter and Line Space**, and **Alignment** are the options of tools you can use to work on your text design.

To edit individual text, click on the text and click **ungroup** at the top right hand corner. You can do a lot here, for instance, you can curve them or rotate them. When you are done, right click on the text and click **group**.

Shapes. Click **Shape** to insert shapes into your design. There are shapes like circles, lines, hearts, squares, triangles and so on.

Upload. Click **Upload** to your designs or images from your device or computer. You can either click **browse** to locate the file from your device or computer or drag and drop into the canvas. You can only upload files in the following formats: **.jpg, .gif, .png, .bmp, .dxf and .svg**.

After uploading a file, you will be required to select an image. Then click on **Continue**. You can also edit the pattern or erase the background. The tools available are **Wand, Eraser** and **Crop**.

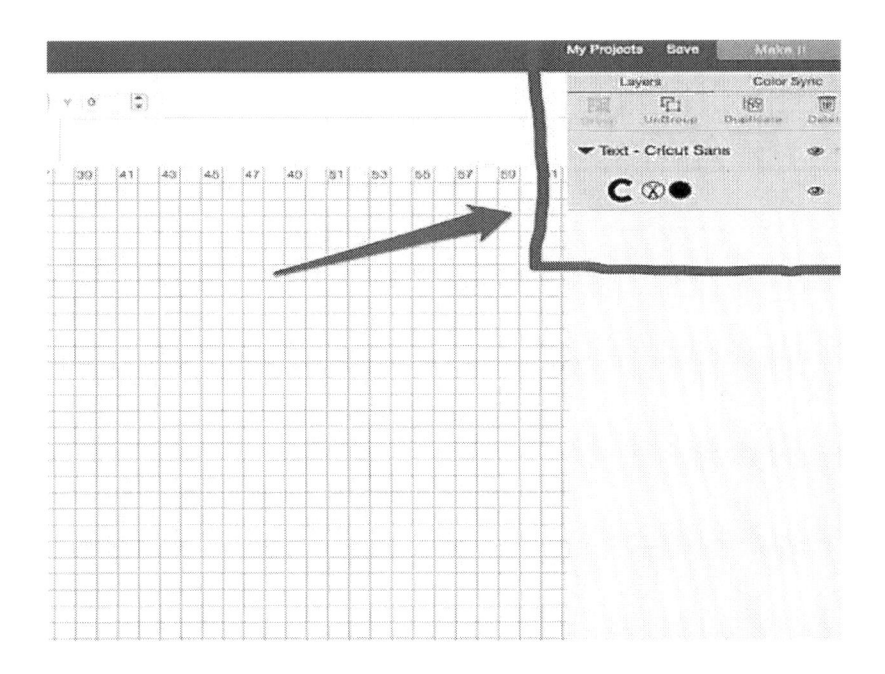

Under the green **Make It** button is the **Layers** menu and **Color Sync.** Click **Layers** and you will see options to **slice, weld, attach, flatten,** and **Contour**. Explore these options based on your intended design. This guide will show you more on some of the options in the next chapter.

Making Use of Sure Cuts A Lot

Sure Cuts A Lot (SCAL) is a popular software, like the Cricut Design Space, which instructs your electronic cutting machine to cut any shape, font, files in **.svg** format and more. It is also used for creating artwork, decals and shapes as you wish to design them. It was first released in 2008 by Craft Edge.

Sure Cuts A Lot doesn't work with Cricut machines anymore. Old versions might still do, but the latest version of Sure Cuts

A Lot are no more compatible with the current 3 Cricut machines – Cricut Maker 3, Cricut Explore 3 and Cricut Joy.

Sure Cuts A Lot still works with the following popular electronic vinyl cutters:

- GCC
- Silhouette SD
- Silhouette Curio
- USCutter
- BlackCat Cougar and Lynx
- Foison
- VinylExpress
- Roland
- Bosskut Gazelle
- SilverBullet
- Craftwell eCraft
- Pazzles Inspiration
- Silhouette CAMEO and Portrait

Craft Edge, the maker of the Sure Cuts A Lot, states in their tutorial for using SCAL versions 3 and 4, that you can use the newest version of SCAL to cut on Cricut machines by sending it to the Version 2. This means you will have to install both Version 2 and their recent version.

The tutorial also states that the version 2 of the Sure Cuts A Lot only supports the Cricut Cake, Cricut Create, Cricut Expression and the Cricut Expression machines. These are older Cricut machines.

The bottomline is that if you intend to use Sure Cut A Lot software with your Cricut Maker 3, you will need to install two versions of the software, version 2 and a most recent version. The latest version when installed will not erase or update the older one. You will have them as two separate applications. So when you are done with designing on the latest version, you will then send to the version 2; which will then instruct your machine to cut the design.

It is noteworthy that the Design Space app or software accepts **.svg** files. It is then an alternative, that your designs saved in **.svg** formats on Sure Cuts A Lot can be uploaded into the Design Space. This might be a better arrangement if for any reason, you insist on using Sure Cuts A Lot to create your designs.

On your latest version of Sure Cuts A Lot, simply export an SVG. Then open your Design Space and upload it there.

Features of Sure Cuts A Lot

To download Sure Cuts A Lot, go to Craft Edge's website (craftedge.com) and log in with your name and software serial number. The CD copy of Sure Cuts A Lot software is only available for Windows computers. It is not clear why this is so. However, Mac computer users can simply download from their website and they are good to go.

The following are the features of the Sure Cuts A Lot software:

- The latest version of Sure Cuts A Lot has newer features such as the brush, stencil tool and freehand utility.
- Compatible with Windows' TrueType and OpenType fonts.
- It can import **.pdf, .svg, .eps, .wpc,** and **.dxf** files.
- It can be used by Windows and Mac OSX computer users.
- Free technical support from Craft Edge, the maker of the software
- What you see is what you cut interface.
- It can select styles such as Shadows, Blackout etc
- It can weld together overlapping letters and shapes
- It has drawing tools to draw and cut.
- It can automatically convert images for cutting. Auto tracing feature.
- It can save and share designs.
- And so on.

Using Design Space

Basically, the Design Space is the software used to design on the Cricut Maker 3. The Design Maker is free of charge. It is available for Windows and Mac computer users and the mobile version is available for use for phone and tablet users with the Android and iOS operating systems.

The Design Space has a library of ready-to-make projects with access to lots of free designs, images and fonts. You can also purchase others. The Design Space allows you to upload your own designs and images in the following acceptable formats - **.jpg, .gif, .png, .bmp, .dxf and .svg**.

Refer to Chapter 3 to find your version of the Design Space.

The Design Space will allow you to create new designs, upload your own, use designs from Cricut Access and instruct your Cricut machine to either write, foil, cut, emboss, engrave, score or perforate the designs.

However, if you are having an issue with your Design Space, you can also reset it. To do this, follow the steps below:

> **Step 1:** Locate the **LocalData** folder and select all the files there. To be sure of selecting all that is there, use the keyboard combination by pressing **Ctrl key + A key.**
>
> **Step 2:** Afterwards, use the keyboard combination **Shift + Delete** keys to permanently remove everything in that folder.
>
> **Step 3:** Now, open **Design Space** for Desktop.
>
> **Step 4:** From the System menu, click **Force Reload**

This should resolve the issue and reset Design Space.

Top Panel of the Cricut Design Space

The Top panel of the Cricut Design Space is the tool bar, where there are buttons for manipulating your designs to your taste. You will find working tools such as: **undo/redo, operation, linetype, fill, select/deselect, edit, align, arrange, flip, size, rotate** and more there. You will also find **Layers** and **Color Sync** at the extreme right.

Undo and Redo

The first two buttons are for undoing the last action and for re-doing it. To undo, click the backward arrow while to redo, click the forward arrow.

Operation

Next is the **Operation** button that includes **cut, draw, print then cut**. Draw here can mean to draw with a pen, scoring tip, foil tip, engraving tip, or debossing tip. The **Print to Cut** is used for stickers. The cut, basically, are for cutting wavy or perforation styles. So the **Operation** basically points your machine to what to do.

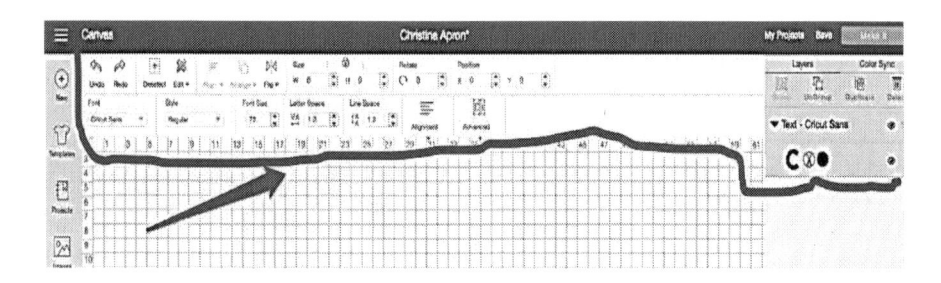

Material Colors

The Material is by default set to black color. You do not need to change this except when you are making more than one object. But if you are making a project with multiple colors of material like the vinyl, you will need to adjust accordingly. It mainly helps to maintain order of which design it cuts first before the next.

Select All or Deselect

When you click the **Select All** button, everything in the canvas is highlighted. Then you can decide what to do with it. For instance, you can reduce or increase the size of whatever is in the canvas, but you will need this button to first select it.

The **deselect** button is to undo the selection. It won't undo the last action, the **Undo** button does that.

Edit

This is where you have the **Linetype, Fill, Size, Rotate, Mirror, Position, Cut, Copy, Paste** and so on. These are tools required to edit your images and text. The **cut** here is the same as the term used in the editing features of your Windows PC. It copies, but makes what you copied to disappear, while it remains temporarily in the clipboard. It is not to be confused with the term used for incising.

You have options of spacing letters or lines, or adjusting the font style and so on, while working on the text.

Offset

This allows you to outline and shadow designs. An outline can be made around text, which can be used for background. Shadows make text look 3-D.

Align

This is used for two or more items. You will need to select the items and click **Align** to ensure they fit together before cutting.

Arrange

This will help you arrange your multiple layers in the order you want. Click the layer and select either **Send to back** or **Send to front** to arrange them in the desired order. To adjust the layers on top or bottom of your design, select either **Move forward** or **Move backward**.

Flip

This helps you to flip horizontally or vertically. If after flipping, it does not appear the way you want it, go back to the first button to undo it.

Size

Use this to re-size an item in your designs. Don't forget to select the item first, so that the software will know what you are asking it to resize. There is a panel there where you can type in the exact size you desire it to be changed to. There is a little lock button there that will ensure that resizing the height changes in proportion to the width. Click the **lock** button to unlock it and input a figure manually.

Rotate

Use this tool to rotate an item as set by default. However, there's room to input the exact degree you would rotate it.

How to Download the Design Space

Follow the steps below to download Cricut Design Space software or app:

Step 1: You need to download the Cricut Design Space. Go to **cricut.com/setup** from your device or PC.

Step 2: Click **Download**

Step 3: locate **Cricut ID** and create an account for yourself.

Step 4: When an account has been created successfully, login into the Design Space software or app.

Step 5: Using Bluetooth or a USB cable, you will then need to connect your Cricut Maker 3 to your PC or device. Plug in your USB cable or turn on your Bluetooth on your device or PC to do so.

Step 6: Then click on **New Product Set-Up** on your Design Space

Step 7: Click **Smart Cutting Machine**

Step 8: Select **Maker 3**. If connection is by USB cable, select **Maker 3: 0 USB**

Step 9: Click **Continue**

Step 10: Follow the prompts afterwards. If you desire sign up for the free trial of Cricut Access, click **Start Free Trial**.

You do not need to subscribe to Cricut Access to start enjoying your dear Cricut Maker 3, it comes with an additional 100 ready-to-make projects. However, since all new machines come with a free trial of Cricut Access for a period of a month, it is recommended that you take advantage of it to enjoy thousands of fonts, images, and project designs. If you are a craft professional or you are currently embarking on a craft project and exhibitions, it is recommended you subscribe to either monthly or annual membership. Don't forget that Premium membership is only available on yearly subscription only, while the Standard membership of Cricut Access can be either monthly or yearly.

Cricut Design Space Top Menu

On the left of the screen of the Cricut Design Space is a menu panel that contains options together with their icons. They are:

New, Templates, Projects, Images, Text, Shapes, Upload

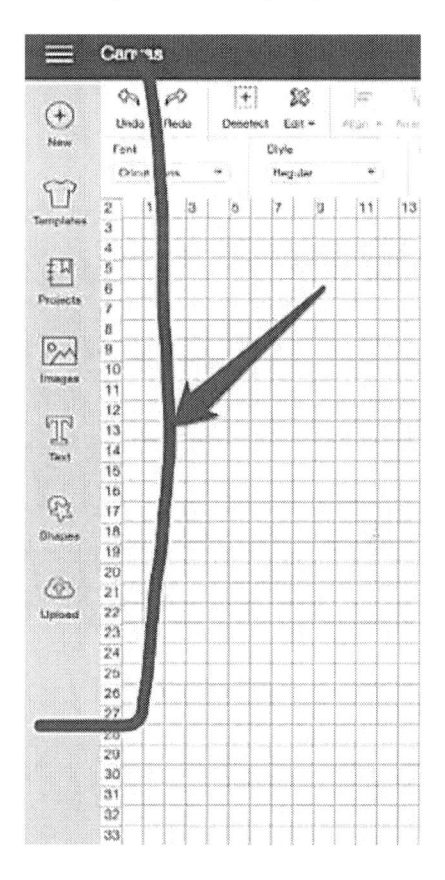

New. Click New if you want to start a **New project**. A blank screen will appear when you do. You will then be instructed to either save your current project or overwrite it with the new one you just opened. Here you have all the tools to help you create a new design.

Templates. Click here to have ready-made designs that you can modify to your taste. You can modify the size, space and type. This is like a short cut to that design you have in mind.

Projects. This is where to click to enter Cricut Access where all the ready-to-make designs are. The designs are ready, just select and make them. However, you can customize them to further suits what you have in mind. You can click on **Categories** to see a drop down menu of several options to select from. There are free ones, you will see them all grouped in a page if you select Free from the menu.

Images. When you are designing and you wish to insert an image on the canvas, click image. This will bring out thousands of images you can select from and to start working your design on. Because of the number of images, you can use the search bar to search for an image quickly. When searching, you can use Filters to further help you narrow down your search.

Then there is the **Linetype**, which has the following depending on the blade or pen inserted:

- Cut
- Draw
- Score

- Engrave
- Deboss
- Wave
- Perf
- Foil – Fine, Medium or Bold

You can also change the **Pen Type** by clicking on it. As you select the pen you wish to use, there will be changes in the image on the canvas.

If you intend to print your cut image, click **Fill**. A drop-down menu will appear, select **Print**. There is a little box beside **Fill** that when you click it, you can change the color of your image.

You can also change the pattern from the **Print Type** small window or click **Edit Pattern** at the bottom of that small window.

The size or scale of the image can be modified by sliding the slider either left or right in the **Edit Pattern** small window. The images can also be rotated here or flipped to either side.

The material color for a cut image can be changed. If two colors are chosen for two images, the machine will cut them in different mats. If you want to cut in the same mat, then ensure the material colors are the same.

Text. Click **Text** and you should be able to type in whatever you desire on the canvas. Texts can be edited from the options at the top left corner of the **Text** screen. **Font, Font**

Style, Font Size, Letter and Line Space, and **Alignment** are the options of tools you can use to work on your text design.

To edit individual text, click on the text and click **Ungroup** at the top right hand corner. You can do a lot here, for instance, you can curve them or rotate them. When you are done, right click on the text and click **group**.

Shapes. Click **Shape** to insert shapes into your design. There are shapes like circles, lines, hearts, squares, triangles and so on.

Upload. Click **Upload** to your designs or images from your device or computer. You can either click **browse** to locate the file from your device or computer or drag and drop into the canvas. You can only upload files in the following formats: **.jpg, .gif, .png, .bmp, .dxf and .svg**. After uploading a file, you will be required to select an image. Then click on **Continue**. You can also edit the pattern or erase the background. The tools available are **Wand, Eraser** and **Crop.**

Uploading Images to Design Space

At the bottom left of the Design Space screen where the menu is, click **Upload** to import files containing your designs or images from your device or computer.

You can either click **browse** to locate the file from your device or computer or drag and drop into the canvas. You can only upload files in the following formats: **.jpg, .gif, .png, .bmp, .dxf and .svg**.

After uploading a file, you will be required to select an image. Then click on **Continue**.

Spacing of Letters

You will want the letters in your text well-spaced before you cut, so that it will result in a mess. It is much of a hassle when cutting paper and cardstock, and spacing letters might be unnecessary. However, if you are cutting vinyl or iron-on, it is very important you space it well before you start cutting. Eliminating space between letters is also called Kerning.

To space your letters, follow the steps below:

Step 1: Type the words and select the font to use

Step 2: Afterwards, ungroup the text by selecting the **text box,** then click **Ungroup** to letters. This will make each letter to be edited or moved around.

Step 3: Fix the spacing issues noticed. For script fonts, you may need to let it overlap a little before welding.

Step 4: Then you must either attach or weld for the letters to be as arranged otherwise, it will scatter. For Script font, just weld, because if you don't, the overlapping letters will end up being cut out separately.

How to Weld

You must have noticed that welding or attaching is the last step in the spacing of letters. To weld or to attach on your Design Space are two different things, but both help keep your design intact on the canvas, so that they are not scattered. Section 6.13 will guide you on how to attach.

To weld is to glue together or fuse together items so that they become one item. It will remove the cut lines between images, or texts.

Follow these steps below to weld, using a script font as an example:

> **Step 1:** On your Design Space canvas, type a word after adding a text box. (Choose a script font)
>
> **Step 2:** Click on the text box to select; then click **Ungroup to letters**.
>
> **Step 3:** Drag the letters close to each other so that they connect each other. This will remove the gap between them.
>
> When you have such letters as **e** or **o** shaded black, this means that the letter connected next to it is too close. So it is important to undo it and adjust it appropriately so that it is corrected. You can make the letters bigger, so that you can see clearly. When you

are done, you can then reduce it back to the original size.

Step 4: For script fonts, don't attach. If you do, the connecting point where the letters overlap will still cut and mess up the project. So in this step, you will weld. When you weld, your Cricut machine will cut the whole word in one piece.

How to Slice

If you know how to slice, you will be able to cut one shape out of another one. You can also cut text from a shape. Each one of the new shape will appear as individual layer in the Layers panel. The highest number of layers you can slice at a time is two. Multi Layered images can be ungrouped so that the slice tool can then be used.

For texts, if you ungroup it from its shadows layer, you will not be able to use the slice tool. It will assume it's an image, unless you ungroup it to individual letters.

To learn how to slice on the Design Space, follow the steps below:

Step 1: Put your images in such a way that they are overlapping

Step 2: Select the images

If you are selecting on Windows or Mac computers, press and hold down the **Ctrl key** while clicking the images one at a time. Each of the layers will be highlighted in the Layers panel. The Slice tool will be activated if two layers are selected.

If you are using an Android or iOS device, tap on the screen and drag a selection box around both layers. This will select both images. Then press **Actions** at the bottom of the screen. Then you can use the slice tool.

Step 3: click **Slice**. The images will appear sliced. Hidden layers will no longer be there in the Layers panel.

Step 4: Continue to slice and layer your images as desired, separate the layers to see your new sliced shapes.

On Windows and Mac computers, when you slice, there will be duplicates, you can edit the images one at a time or delete unwanted ones. On Android and iOS devices, they won't be duplicated.

How to Flatten

Remember that there are five basic tools used to work with layers in the Design Space. Apart from the **Slice, Weld, Attach** and **Contour, Flatten** is one.

The Flatten tool is used for flattening more than one image into one Print layer so that the **Print then Cut** can now be used. It removes internal cut lines so that makes them one layer, and then get them ready as a single Print image to be cut. The Flatten tool will prevent your design from being sliced into pieces. When the Flatten tool has completed its job, there would be just one layer, and then the **Print then Cut** feature can now print your multi-colored image.

How to Attach

As earlier mentioned, **Attach** is different from **Weld**. While Weld makes shapes as one, **Attach** only keeps them together. **Attach** is like a paper clip.

Attach will keep layers together and keep your project intact on the canvas, but **Detach** will separate them. **Attach** will keep its formatted form when sent to the mat for cutting.

Follow the steps below to attach in the Cricut Design Space:

> **Step 1:** Select the images or text you want to attach by drawing a selection box around your project. You can also select by holding down the **Shift key** on your keyboard and then click on the layer one by one.
>
> **Step 2:** Click the paper clip icon at the bottom right corner of your screen to attach.
>
> **Step 3:** After attaching, the **Attach** layer will appear at the top of the Layers Panel. The next thing to do is to

click **Make It.** This will send your project to the cutting mat the exact same layout as it is on the canvas.

Note that if you can't attach, you might need to ungroup the selected layer first.

How to Group or Ungroup

Basically, the **Group** tool makes you gather several layers or items and make them seem like one, but they are each still individual items. This will allow you to move, edit or do whatever with the grouped items at once. Whenever you want to work with only one of the items, you will use the **Ungroup** tool to separate them. Use the **Group** tool to keep multi-colored and multi-layered projects together on your canvas.

It is important to note that, unlike the **Attach** tool, **Group** tool will not keep your project intact on the mat.

Do the following to group or ungroup a text:

> **Step 1:** To edit individual text, click on the text and click **Ungroup** at the top right hand corner. You can do a lot here, for instance, you can curve them or rotate them.
>
> **Step 2:** When you are done, right click on the text and click **group**.

The same method applies to grouping and ungrouping layers. To select layers, simply hold down the **Shift key** on your keyboard and click each layer you want to group. Then click **Group** to group them together.

How to duplicate designs on Cricut Design Space

You can create more copies of the same design on your Cricut Design Space. To do this, follow the steps below:

Step 1: Go to the **Project Preview** screen on your Design Space

Step 2: If you are using **Windows or Mac computers**, you will see the **Project Copies** field, choose the desired number of copies you want your designed to be duplicated to. Or simply use the arrow beside it to increase the number.

On iOS, go to **Mat settings icon** at the upper left corner. Then tap the **Project Copies** field to put in the number of copies you want duplicated. Then click **done** to effect changes.

On Android, locate the mat settings icon at the upper left corner to click on it. Then tap the **Project Copies** field to put in the number of copies you want duplicated. Then click **done** to effect changes.

Step 3: Smart Materials or Mats will be added to the **Project Preview** immediately.

How to Delete Uploaded Images from Cricut Design Space

There are two ways to remove your uploaded images from the Design Space application.

For the first method, follow the steps below to delete:

Step 1: Launch the Design Space app

Step 2: Open a new project

Step 3: Click **Upload** from the bottom of the left menu

Step 4: The upload screen will appear with your most recent images. Locate **View All** and click on it to show all your uploaded images in the image library.

Step 5: Select the uploaded you wish removed.

Step 6: Then click on **i** appearing in a circle at the bottom of the selected image.

Step 7: A small screen will appear where you will click **Delete.**

Step 8: Confirm your selection by clicking **Yes** at the top of the screen. Your uploaded image will be deleted.

For the second method, follow the steps below to delete:

Step 1: On your Design Space's canvas, go to **images**

Step 2: Then click browse all images

Step 3: From the options, locate **ownership** and select **uploaded** from there. Your images will then appear

Step 4: Select the uploaded you wish removed.

Step 5: Then click on **i** appearing in a circle at the bottom of the selected image.

Step 6: A small screen will appear where you will click **Delete**

Step 7: Confirm your selection by clicking **Yes** at the top of the screen. Your uploaded image will be deleted.

How to Color Sync

The basic function of the Color Sync in Design Space is to allow you to match colors of a project so that you can reduce the number of different materials you intend to use. The Color Sync will definitely save you time and materials. The Color Sync panel will only display the layers set to cut and it will not show the Print layer or Write Layer or Score Layer.

To learn how to use color sync in Design Space, follow the simple steps below:

Step 1: in the right hand of the Design Space screen, open the Color Sync panel.

Step 2: Then drag and drop each image into the layer you want synchronized to. Then they will all be the same exact color.

Getting Started with Text

On your Design Space screen, click **Text** and you should be able to type in whatever you desire on the canvas. Texts can be edited from the options at the top left corner of the Text screen. **Font, Font Style, Font Size, Letter and Line Space,** and **Alignment** are the options of tools you can use to work on your text design.

To edit individual text, click on the text and click **Ungroup** at the top right hand corner. You can do a lot here, for instance, you can curve them or rotate them. When you are done, right click on the text and click **group**.

Other things, apart from adding a text to a project, grouping and ungrouping, that you can do with text in your Design Space application are using script fonts, welding, attaching, curving text around a shape or circle, fixing spaces on script fonts, and changing the pattern and color fill.

How to Edit Images in Cricut Design Space Using the Slice Tool

The Slice tool can be used in Cricut Design Space to split images. You may want to split images to cut a shape out of an image or photo, or to create a monogram.

Follow the steps below to learn how to use the slice tool to edit images in Cricut Design Space.

Step 1: Click on **New Project** and then click on **Upload** when the canvas appears.

Step 2: click **Upload Image**. Browse the location of your file and click **Open**.

Step 3: Click on the just uploaded image, then click the green **Insert Images** button.

Step 4: On the menu on the left, click **Shape**. Select **Square**. Click on the **padlock** icon to unlock it so that you can drag it to become a rectangle.

Step 5: Afterwards, drag the rectangle on the image and put it where you would want it split. The rectangle should be bigger than the width of your image.

Step 6: Right click on the rectangle and click **Duplicate**. A copy of the rectangle will be created, which should be set aside for now.

It is very important to note that if the uploaded image is multi-layered in **.svg** format, then you should ungroup it first. Simply select all the layers and click **Ungroup**.

Step 7: Now, select the image together with the rectangle. Then click **Align** and choose **Center** from the options. The rectangle will move to the center of the image and across it.

Step 8: Then click **Weld** while the two layers are still selected.

Step 9: Now go to the second rectangle, we earlier duplicated (step 6). Right click on it and select **Send to Front.**

Step 10: Then go to **Align** and then select **Center**, like you did with the first rectangle. You can have the rectangle positioned anywhere you want.

Step 11: Select both the rectangle and the image and click **Slice.**

Step 12: You can delete on the pieces of the layers that have been sliced, by clicking on them and pressing the **delete icon** or **delete button** in the **Layers panel.**

Step 13: As earlier done (Step 4), create a new rectangle and put it over the bottom half of the image. Select both the rectangle and the image and again, press **Slice**. Remove the pieces you don't need after slicing. Meanwhile, the pieces of the images are now split from each other and it will reflect in the Layers panel. Each layer can be moved around as much as you want.

Step 14: If it is in line with your design, you can add some text. You can then get it ready to be cut on your Cricut Maker 3.

How to Access Special Characters

In the Cricut Design Space, it is possible to open and use special characters and fonts such as the glyphs, font extras, dingbats, swirls, ornaments, curls and so on. Accents and flourishes (like the Yoruba language or Spanish language characters) and the degree symbol can be used in Cricut Design Space on Windows computers by using Character Map.

How to Add Accents to Fonts

A Character Map app usually comes pre-installed on Windows PC, but for whatever reason you cannot find it on yours, you can find it in Microsoft Store. Or you can simply download it here:

https://www.microsoft.com/en-us/p/character-map-uwp/9wzdncrdxf41

You will then copy and paste the glyphs into the Cricut Design Space.

How to Add Accents to Fonts

In the Cricut Design Space, you can also add accents. The Character Map app will come in handy here too. Most of the fonts usually have symbols and accents added to them. Follow these simple steps to do so:

Step 1: Go to the Character Map app, locate the font you wish to use and click on the letter with accent. Then click on the **Copy icon** on the far right.

Step 2: Now back to Cricut Design Space, ensure the same font is chosen from the dropdown menu. Then insert a new text box.

Step 3: Use your keyboard shortcut **Ctrl + V keys** to paste the letter with an accent.

How to Add Flourishes to Fonts

Follow the steps below to add Flourishes to your Fonts in the Cricut Design Space:

Step 1: In the Cricut Design Space, open a text box and select the font you desire to use.

Step 2: Then go to your Character Map app and locate the name of the font. Under the same font, look for the extra character you wish to add and then click on it. Then use your keyboard shortcut keys **Ctrl + C** to copy it.

Step 3: Return to the Cricut Design Space screen and paste it into the text box, which can be done with keyboard shortcut keys **Ctrl + V.** Then character will show up and you can then continue typing and working on your project.

How to Add a Degree Symbol to Text

Again, we will use the Character Map, because it is faster. However, there is another method, which is by uploading 2 oval images and slicing them to create a degree symbol.

To use the Character Map app, follow the steps below to add a degree symbol to your project in the Cricut Design Space:

Step 1: In the Cricut Design Space, open a text box and select **Arial** font. Arial usually has the extra characters and symbols than other fonts.

Step 2: Then go to your Character Map app and locate Arial. Under it, look for the degree symbol and then click on it. Then use your keyboard shortcut keys **Ctrl + C** to copy it.

Step 3: Return to the Cricut Design Space screen and paste it into the text box, which can be done with keyboard shortcut keys **Ctrl + V**. Then character will show up and you can then continue typing and working on your project.

How to Curve a Text

The Curve tool is used to bend or curve text into circular form in your Design Space. It is located right above the canvas in the Edit toolbar as earlier discussed. It is only presently available on the Cricut Design Space version for the Windows and Mac computers. It is not on the Android and iOS version.

To curve a text on your Design Space application using your PC, follow the steps below:

> **Step 1:** On the menu on the left of the canvas of the Design Space, click **Text**.
>
> **Step 2:** Type something into the textbox.
>
> **Step 3:** Select a font, font style and adjust the letter spacing with the Letter Space tool.
>
> In case you have more than one line of text, enter each line into a separate textbox. Alternatively, you can use the **Ungroup** to Lines to separate the lines to different textboxes.
>
> **Step 4:** Then click the **Curve** tool, a slider and a diameter field with numbers will appear.
>
> **Step 5:** Use the slider to determine how you would like to have it curved. The diameter number field changes as you drag the slider.

Please note that you can edit curved text unless they are flattened or welded. Text that has been ungrouped to individual letters and the grouped back cannot be curved by the **Curve** tool.

How to Make a Stencil

There are many methods of making stencils with your Cricut Maker 3 machine. They give good finishes to home decors, t-shirts, wooden signs and so on. Stencils are designs cut out of thin sheets of plastic, vinyl or paper. Basically, stencils are applied in such a way that they are laid on the surface you wish to design and then you apply paint to pass through the areas you have cut out as a form of design.

What You Can Make with Stencils

You can make the following using stencils:

- Painted floor
- Durative painted wall
- Wall tiles
- Wood signs
- Glass etching
- Cake decorating
- Wallpapers
- Silk screen printing
- Cookies decoration
- And so on

Materials Required to Make Stencils

When making stencils, there are some materials you should have ready, such as:
- Cricut stencil vinyl
- Cricut Maker 3
- A smooth surface such as a wooden tray or a smooth pavement.
- Transfer tape
- Chalk Paint or any paint or stain
- Brush – stencil brush or sponge brush
- Scraper tool
- Brayer
- Weeding tools
- And so on.

Making Stencils with Your Cricut Machine

Follow the steps below to make stencils with your Cricut cutting machine:

Step 1: Design the stencil. Select the image to use to make your stencil either from the Cricut Access Library, or by uploading a **.svg** file. You can as well just make a new stencil using the Cricut Design Space.

There are thousands of patterns and stencils in the Cricut Access, so it's best to just use the search to find the one you like. You can find good free stencils from **etsy.com** and **freestencilgallery.com**, which you can then upload. Creating a stencil on Design Space is pretty easy; but keep all the parts of the stencil connected so that you can cut the stencil as one piece.

Step 2: Time to cut your stencil. Once the design is done, you can now get ready to cut. If you are cutting a stencil vinyl, you will use either a StandardGrip or LightGrip mat. Use the brayer tool to make sure the material is smoothly laid and stuck onto the mat.

Press the button to insert the mat into the cutting machine.

Step 3: On your Cricut Design Space, at the upper top corner and click **Make It**.

On the Prepare screen, click **continue** after checking that all is correct and well set.

Then the Make screen will appear, where you will click **Browse All Materials** and pick **Stencil Vinyl**.

Step 4: Cross check that the blade is Fine Point Blade and that it is correctly inserted. Then press the **Go** button so that your Cricut machine can start cutting. Remove the mat when the cutting task is done.

Step 5: Remove the mat after cutting.

Step 6: At this point, you might need to weed with the transfer tape the design if your design is intricate and has floating elements.

Nevertheless, if your design is not complex and has connecting elements, you will not need weeding and will not need the transfer tape.

Follow these steps if you need to weed and use transfer tape to transfer stencil from the liner to your working surface:-

1. Using a tweezer or weeding tool, remove the negative pieces from the stencil.
2. Put the sticky part of the transfer tape down on the stencil design. Then rub the transfer tape on the stencil vinyl smoothly.
3. Then remove the stencil vinyl liner at the angle of 45 degree.
4. Finally, gently put the transfer tape with the stencil vinyl on the surface.

Step 7: At this point you need to apply the Stencil. Follow the steps below to do so:

1. Gently place the stencil vinyl on a clean and dry surface you want to work with, in the exact position you will want it to appear when done.
2. Rub the stencil vinyl on the surface with a Cricut scraper. To avoid bubbles, start from the middle towards the edge. If you are using the transfer tape, you should rub or burnish the same way.

Step 8: Use your brush to dab the paint on the stencil vinyl. You can use a sponge brush or a stencil brush.

The paint will follow the design of the cut out parts of the stencil to transfer it to the surface of the project material.

Remove the stencil vinyl when it is dry. You can re-use the stencil vinyl again on a new surface. For instance, if you are transferring a stencil vinyl design on 20 t-shirts, you will keep repeating the process until you have completed the transfer to the 20 t-shirts. Although it is possible your stencil spoils as you continue to use it several times, you can simply make a new one on your Cricut machine by following the steps above over again.

How to Use Contour

The Contour tool is one of the tools in the Edit toolbar. It allows a portion of an image to be hidden simply by removing unwanted cut lines.

Follow the steps below to use contour tool with text in your Cricut Design Space:

Step 1: If the image or text has multiple layers, then ungroup it.

Step 2: Then select the layer you want to remove the cut lines and click **Contour** in the Layers panel using Windows or Mac computers. On Android and iOS, click **Hide Contour** from the **Actions Menu**.

Step 3a: On Windows or Mac computers, click on the cut line (the lines on the image is the individual cut line) you want hidden. To indicate that it is hidden, it will change to a lighter shade. You can repeat this with other lines you want hidden.

Step 3b: On Android or iOS devices, the dark grey lines are the individual cut lines. Click on the cut line you want hidden. To indicate that it is hidden, it will change to a lighter shade. You can repeat this with other lines you want hidden.

Step 4: Close the **Hide Contour** window.

Please note that you can bring back the cut lines from being hidden. Follow the above steps to do so, but click on the hidden lines to restore.

CHAPTER SEVEN

Vinyl for Cricut Projects

With the vinyls you can birth several projects such as labels, decals, customized gift items, home decor and so on. There is a wide range of colors to select from, as well, to give the exact visual you envisaged to your craft.

There are two main types of vinyl, which are:

1. Adhesive vinyl
2. Iron-on vinyl

Adhesive Vinyls are sticky on one side. Removable and Permanent vinyls are some types of adhesive vinyls, though the permanent can be removed when hot heat is used and it is scraped off. You can adhesive vinyl on walls, tumblers, windows, glass and so on. If applied on hot surfaces such as the microwave, it will peel off.

Follow these simple steps to apply adhesive vinyl:

Step 1: Place the vinyl on the StandardGrip mat facing up.

Step 2: Then use Design Space to cut images out on your Cricut machine

Step 3: Finally use the transfer tape to transfer your design on the surface of your project.

Iron-on Vinyls are generally known as Heat Transfer Vinyls (HTV). Iron-on is Cricut's preferred term. Unlike Adhesive Vinyls, they use heat so that they can adhere to your project materials, especially wood and some fabric. This is the vinyl to use for tshirts, totes, shoes, and so on.

The following steps are the general method of using Iron-on vinyls:

> **Step 1:** Cut iron-on vinyls on **Mirror setting**. This is because heat will be applied on the plastic side so that the vinyl can be transferred into the material.
>
> **Step 2:** On the **Prepare** screen on the Design Space, click on **Mirror** setting
>
> **Step 3:** Then set it to cut on your Cricut machine and weed.
>
> **Step 4:** Transfer the cut vinyl face down, applying heat on the plastic side to melt the vinyl on the surface.

The following are the different types of Cricut vinyls –

- Cricut Holographic Vinyl,
- Premium Outdoor Glossy vinyl,
- Glitter vinyl,
- Cricut Vinyl Dry Erase,
- Cricut Printable Vinyl and
- Cricut Vinyl Chalkboard.

Vinyl Tricks

The following are a few tips to note when using vinyl:

- To avoid waste, don't cut a sheet off your vinyl when placing it on the mat, rather leave it on the roll like that.
- Place the transfer tape on your adhesive vinyl and rub smoothly on the surface of project material with a scraper or spatula.
- For iron-on vinyl, transfer the cut iron-on vinyl on your material by applying heat on the plastic side. The design will melt and stick to the material.

Using the Cricut Transfer Tape

The Cricut Transfer Tape is sticky on one side. It is the perfect accessory for removing debris and dust from most of the cutting mats, especially the FabricGrip mat that usually has more dirt. It can also be used in cutting and applying vinyl.

Follow the steps below on how to cut and apply vinyl using the Cricut Transfer Tape:

Step 1: put the vinyl liner on the side down onto your mat. Use StandardGrip mat

Step 2: Select images and adjust the size. Then put the mat into your Cricut machine.

Step 3: Do machine settings

Step 4: Press the **Go** button on your machine.

Step 5: Use weeding tools to remove the negative pieces from the images. Leave the clear liner intact.

Step 6: Start preparation with the transfer tape by removing the tape liner.

Step 7: Put the sticky part of the Transfer Tape over the images gently. Start from the center towards the edges to prevent bubbles. Use a scraper to rub the tape onto the vinyl very well.

Step 8: Then, remove the vinyl liner at an angle of 45 degrees.

Step 9: Gently place the Transfer Tape with the vinyl images onto your project surface. Ensure it is well set.

Step 10: Starting from the middle, use a scraper to rub the Transfer Tape on the project surface.

Step 11: Carefully remove the Transfer Tape at an angle of 45 degrees from the surface. Ensure you rub the Transfer Tape on the surface very well before you peel off.

How to Layer vinyl

There are two methods to layer your iron-on vinyls. First method is by slicing it and the other one is to layer the vinyl on top of each other without slicing.

First Method –

This method is also known as the Knockout method.

Here you use the slice tool and arrange together the pieces of vinyl cut out by the machine.

Second Method – Iron-on

Follow the steps below to layer vinyl without using the slice tool:

Step 1: Launch Design Space, make or upload a design. Insert additional images needed.

Step 2: Layer the images on how you want them to appear on your material, such as t-shirt, cap, etc.

Step 3: Click **Group** to separate them and then resize them.

Step 4: Click **Make It.**

Step 5: Click the **Mirror setting** for every mat chosen and adjust color.

Step 6: Click **Continue** then choose the type of material.

Step 7: Place the shiny side of the iron-on down

Step 8: Set to cut, and weed the excess after cutting.

Step 9: Layer them to fit them together.

Step 10: Transfer them to your material by starting with the bottom layer first. To transfer, use a heat press to press the material down to it. Then wait for it to cool and remove the plastic side.

Step 11: Repeat the process with the next layer until you are done.

These types of iron on are good as top layer, especially for the second method:

- Foil iron-on
- Glitter iron-on
- Patterned iron-on
- Holographic iron-on

Iron-on Wood Wall

The normal adhesive vinyl does not adhere well to many surfaces like wood. Therefore, this is where the iron-on vinyls are very handy, especially as you will have to bypass the use of transfer tape. The process is simple – cut your design by sending from the Design Space to your Cricut machine and iron on it on your project material.

Follow the steps below to do this for a wood wall project:-

Step 1: Cut the wood block to your desired size for the wall you wish to place it. Then paint it for a background color and let it dry completely.

Step 2: On Design Space, resize your image to the block size

Step 3: Cut the the iron-on on your Cricut machine

Step 4: Next is to weed the cut out image

Step 5: To apply the iron-on to the wood block, use the EasyPress tool.

Step 6: Peel off the clear film

Step 7: Then drill hole in the back of the wood block so that it can be nailed to the wall.

Weeding iron-on Vinyl

Weeding is the process of removing excess pieces after cutting materials on your Cricut machine. Iron-on material will also leave behind waste on your mat after a machine cut.

Weeding iron-on vinyl is simple and straightforward, because you only need to pull hard the plastic at the back. Do the following to weed your iron-on vinyl:

- Pull off the larger chunks of unused iron-on
- Use a weeding tool or pointer to pick out smaller pieces
- You can scratch a little to remove tough ones, but you should do so carefully.
- Thrash the weeded waste.

Applying Iron-on Vinyl

Now that you have cut your iron-on vinyl and you have also weeded it, it is time to apply it.

Follow the steps below to do so:

Step 1: Place the design where you want it on your material and let the plastic side of the iron-on design face up.

Step 2: Put the Cricut protective sheet or any thin fabric on the iron-on to cover everything to protect the vinyl and the fabric from the heat of the iron. It also helps re-distribute heat evenly all over the design.

Step 3: Use EasyPress to press down the design under the fabric or protective sheet. You can also use a dry pressing iron. Ensure that the vinyl stuck.

Step 4: Then peel off the whole plastic at the back and let it cool completely.

Design Space Software Secrets and the Design Space App

The Design Space is a free software on Windows or Mac computers or apps on Android or iOS devices used together with Cricut cutting machines. In the software or app, you will have access to numerous fonts, images and template projects. The Chromebook or Unix/Linix computers do not enjoy support from Design Space.

Below are the system requirements for each of the operating system supported:

Computers:

Windows	Mac
Windows 8 minimum	MacOS 10.15 minimum
CPU 2 core or equivalent AMD processor	1.83 GHz CPU
Minimum of 4 GB RAM	Minimum of 4 GB RAM
Minimum of 2 GB free space on disk	Minimum of 2 GB free space on disk
USB or Bluetooth	USB or Bluetooth
1024 x 768 px screen resolution – minimum display	1024 x 768 px screen resolution – minimum display
Broadband internet connection	Broadband internet connection
For download, 2-3 Mbps minimum	For download, 2-3 Mbps minimum
For uploads, 1-2 Mbps minimum	For uploads, 1-2 Mbps minimum
Design Space for Desktop is available	Design Space for Desktop is available

| offline | offline |

Please note that Windows 7 PCs are not supported.

To use the feature **offset** in Design Space will require as high as 64-bit Windows 10 and higher MacOS.

Devices:

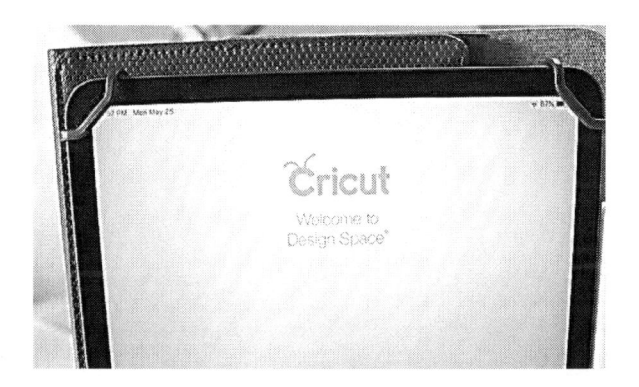

iOS	Android
iOS 14 minimum	Android 8.0 minimum
	Smartphones and tablets only, Chromebooks are not supported
For download, 2 - 3 Mbps minimum	For download, 2-3 Mbps minimum
For uploads, 1 - 2 Mbps minimum	For uploads, 1-2 Mbps minimum

Available offline	Not available offline

Please note the following:

1. You cannot cut with the Knife Blade with the Design Space app. You will need to use Design Space for PC/laptop.
2. You can use the Design Space anywhere as long as there is Internet connection for iOS. You can access any design saved to your Cricut account anywhere in the world.
3. The app has a Make-it-Now gallery from which you can access a vast number of projects.
4. The app has a unique preview feature where you can turn on the camera of your device and point your design to where you want to place the design when you are done. This will make you decide if the design is suitable for the position or there is a need to change the colors.

CHAPTER EIGHT

Cricut Projects

Cricut has an online community called the Cricut Community where thousands of projects are submitted by Cricut users worldwide. You can access these projects too. Perhaps, you may want to add your projects there too for others to access and use. Note however, that the Community project search is not available in the app at the moment, but via a browser.

Searching For a Project

Follow these steps to guide you there:

Step 1: Open the Cricut Design Space on a browser.

Step 2: Sign in with your Cricut ID and your password

Step 3: Go to **Projects**. Click **View All** to land in the Projects screen.

Step 4: From the dropdown menu, click **Cricut Community.**

Step 5: In the search field, type in the key words of the projects you are looking for. You will get thousands of results if you are not descriptive enough.

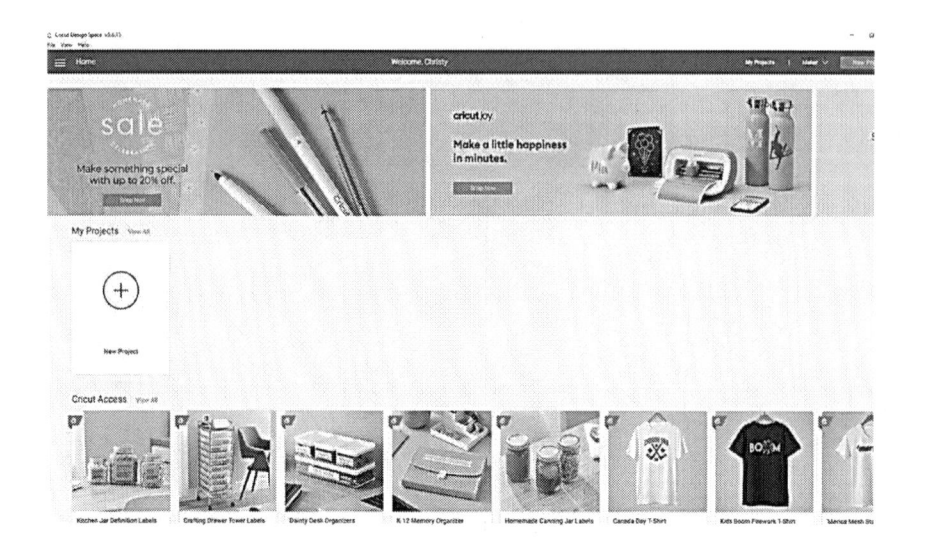

Starting A New Project

Your previously saved projects are listed in **My projects**. Click **View All** to see them all or continue where you stopped.

To start a new project, follow the steps below:

Step 1: Open Design Space

Step 2: Click the new project button or the + symbol under it.

Step 3: A blank canvas will appear where you can start using the menu and the toolbars to work on a design. You can also upload a file of acceptable formats. Or perhaps, click the Cricut Access to access the designs there.

Basically, the Design Space screen is divided into:

- The top toolbar, the menu panel on the left, the canvas area and the layers panel at the top right.

The Canvas is a vast area right in the center of the Design Space screen. It has grids marked with rulers showing their real scale as it is obtainable on your cutting mat.

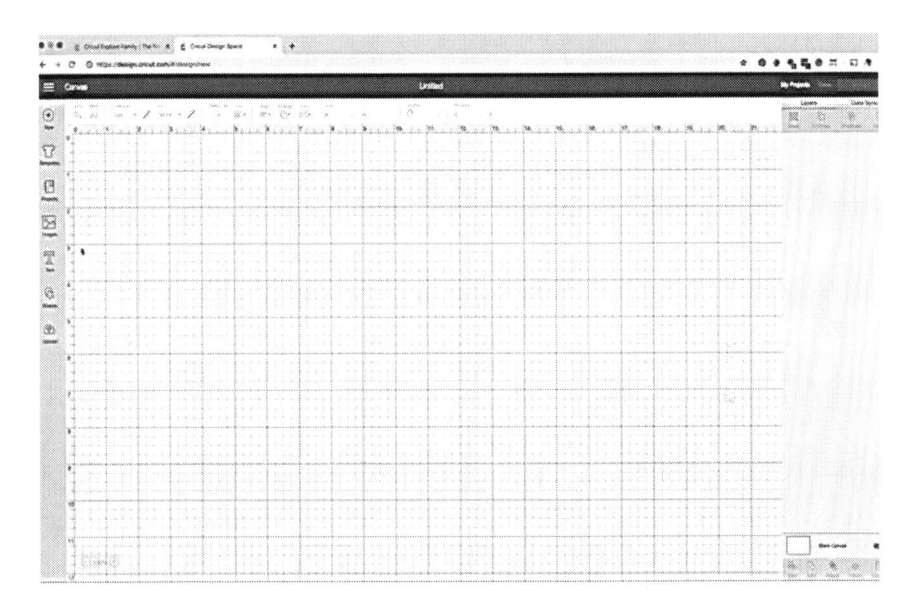

Customized Umbrella (Mickey Mouse Design)

To customize your umbrella with Mickey Mouse design using your Cricut machine, you will need the following:

- Cricut machine
- Clear umbrella
- Cricut Vinyl pack

Follow the steps below to customize your umbrella with Mickey Mouse design using your Cricut machine:

Step 1: Open Design Space. Insert the Balloon image from Cricut Access. Then remove the 2 layers at the top.

Step 2: Click **Shape** on the left menu and add 2 circles to the Balloon image. The two circles are to be used as the ears of the Mickey Mouse.

Step 3: Weld the 3 items so that they become one image. You can copy the welded image to as many as you want and resize them to different sizes so that they fit the screen. Move them around and flip accordingly to do so.

Step 4: Select all the welded images and attach them. This will make the cutting on the mat just as it is on the canvas.

Step 5: Click **Go**. Your vinyl should have been inserted in the mat and then inserted into the machine.

Repeat the above steps to make and cut different colors.

Step 6: After cutting, weed the excess vinyl.

Step 7: Clean the umbrella and apply the vinyl. Since it's a clear transparent umbrella, you can apply the design to the inside of the umbrella so that it can last longer.

Step 8: Leave the umbrella to dry. It's best to leave it out open to dry for at least 24 hours.

Dress Embellishments

You will need the following if you wish to make dress embellishments using your Cricut machine:

- Cricut machine
- A plain dress
- Metallic poster board
- Glue
- Glue gun

Follow the steps below to make a dress embellishment with your Cricut machine:

Step 1: Use flower templates from the Design Space to select from a whole lot of collections there.

Step 2: Resize the flower shapes to different sizes as desired. Make several as possible, at least 100.

Step 3: Then cut all the flowers on the poster board already placed on the mat.

Step 4: After cutting the flower shapes, Use All purpose glue to glue some together to make them thicker and stronger.

Step 5: Heat up the glue gun and begin to attach them to the dress. Alternatively, you can sew the flower shapes to the dress.

Floral Vinyl Wall Decals

To make floral vinyl wall decals using your Cricut machine, you will need the following:

- Cricut machine
- Removable vinyl
- Transfer tape
- Scraper or weeding tool
- Measuring tape

Follow the steps below to make floral vinyl wall decals using your Cricut machine:

Step 1: Look up Design Space to find a good floral image. You can alter any image to suit your taste by using the contour tool.

Step 2: Insert the vinyl in the mat, then set your Cricut machine to cut. Weed afterwards and put the cuts together.

Step 3: Use Transfer Tape to apply the vinyl. You should now apply the vinyl designs to the wall in different, but arranged or random patterns as desired.

Acrylic Keychains

Keychains are good items you can make at home and sell. You can use scraps in making them and you can customize them as gifts to family and friends.

You will need the following materials to make the acrylic keychains:

- Cricut machine
- Permanent vinyl
- Keychain
- Pliers
- Awl
- Transfer Tape
- StandardGrip mat
- Basic tool set

Follow the steps below to make acrylic keychains using your Cricut machine:

Step 1: Open a new project on Design Space. Click Upload on the left menu. Upload your SVG file with the design.

Step 2: Check the Layers panel, should there be any layer you don't want, disable it.

Step 3: Resize your desired layers accordingly and click save. Then click **Make It.**

Step 4: Adjust the settings. Select premium vinyl, Fine Point Blade, default pressure.

Step 5: Then you should cut your design on your Cricut machine. Weed. Then apply the transfer tape. Line it up to the acrylic piece to apply.

If you want your vinyl to stick better, wipe your acrylic round with alcohol.

Step 6: Use a scraper to rub it well to the blank and then gently remove the transfer tape.

Step 7: Push the vinyl through the hole by using the awl and then twist it to create a hole for the keychain ring to pass through.

Step 8: Pass the ring through the hole made in Step 7 using the pliers.

Step 9: With alcohol, wipe the keychain with alcohol to remove fingerprints.

Wood Sign

To make wood sign using your Cricut machine, you will need the following materials:

- Cricut machine

- Plywood or any type of wood.
- Paint
- Paint brushes
- Transfer tape
- Adhesive vinyl
- Scraper or weeding tool
- Picture hanger

Follow the steps below to make wood sign using your Cricut machine:

Step 1: Go to Cricut Design Space and type the words you want on the sign. Select a font and also adjust size. Then insert a suitable image either by uploading or from the Cricut Access or by creating one.

Step 2: Put the vinyl on the mat to use as a stencil. Then cut the text and the image(s).

Step 3: Weed the vinyl that is not relevant to this project. Use the Weeder tool to weed smaller pieces.

Step 4: Prepare your wood. Clean and make sure it is dry.

Step 5: Use the transfer tape to transfer the designs to the wood material. You will need the scraper to burnish the transfer tape so that the vinyl is well stuck to it. Also place the text stencils on the wood.

Step 6: Firmly seal the edges of the text stencils to prevent spillage. Use the brush to paint through all the stencils.

Step 7: Carefully remove the text stencils and the transfer tape.

Step 8: Leave the design to dry; then add a picture hanger at the back of the wood.

Paper Flowers

To make Paper Flowers with the Cricut machine, you will need the following materials:

- Cardstock or Cricut Cardstock
- Cricut machine
- LightGrip mat
- Glue gun

Making paper flowers or rose using the Cricut machine, follow the steps below:

Step 1: Use flower templates from the Design Space to select from a whole lot of collections there.

Step 2: Resize the flower shapes to different sizes as desired.

Step 3: then cut all the flowers on the poster board already placed on the mat.

Step 4: After cutting the flower shapes

Step 5: Heat up the glue gun and begin to attach them to wherever you want them.

You can add glitters to your paper rose, or just paint the tips. You add a whole lot of extra as much as your creativity permits.

Birthday Cake Topper

The Cricut machine can be used to cut out a customized design that can be glued to a skewer, which in turn is inserted into a cake.

Follow the steps below to make a birthday cake topper using your Cricut machine:

Step 1: On the Design Space software, use a good font to type a text. Add some image(s) too, like the picture of the celebrant.

Step 2: Work on the text, you can make them bold, and stretch to widen it. You can do many other things with your text to further personalize the design. You should ensure the font is fat, because of cutting. The letters should overlap or connect with one another. Work on the size of the whole design.

Step 3: Weld the text to ensure it cuts as one piece.

Step 4: Use a poster board on the mat. Then press cut to start cutting on your Cricut machine. You can cut another copy for the back of the skewer.

Step 5: Use the hot glue gun to glue the design on a wooden skewer, both front and back. Done!

You can make it for any occasion – wedding, baptisms, anniversary, matriculation, graduation, and so on.

Flower Corsage

The following are what you will need to make a flower corsage using the Cricut machine:

- Cardstock
- Cricut machine
- Glue
- Scissors
- Ribbons
- pins

Follow the steps below to make flower corsage using the Cricut machine:

Step 1: Use Design Space to print then cut your chosen flower template.

Step 2: After cutting, you can spray the paper with water to make them soft to curl.

Step 3: Use either pin on glue to hold ends of the leaves and then let it dry.

Step 4: Use ribbons if necessary. Finally, wrap the corsage in a cellophane bag.

Leather Hair Accessories

Leather hair accessories can be made in diverse ways. If you are using real leather, then it is recommended you use the Deep Cut blade. Use a normal blade for Faux leather.

To make leather hair accessories with your Cricut machine, you will need the following:

- Cricut machine
- Cricut Faux leather
- Hot Glue gun
- Barrette blanks
- Elastic cord

To make leather hair accessories with your Cricut machine, you will need the following:

Step 1: Open Design Space to create designs, or use a template or upload a file. A flower design, for instance..

Step 2: Edit the image as you desire, especially the size. Do material settings.

Step 3: click **Make It.**

Step 4: Put the leather to the cutting mat and load it into the machine. Press the **Go** button to start cutting.

Step 5: Start from Step 1 again to do make and cut different colors.

Step 6: Measure the elastic cord and attach it from one end of the headband to the other. Apply the hot glue after knotting at the ends. Also use the hot glue to arrange and glue the flowers as desired.

Afterwards, use the hot glue to glue it to the top of the blank barrette.

Leather Journal cover

If you are using real leather, then it is recommended you use the Deep-Cut Blade. Use a normal blade for Faux leather.

You will need the following materials to make Leather journal cover using the Cricut machine:

- Cricut machine
- StandardGrip mat
- Cricut Faux leather
- Iron-on vinyl
- Basic tool set
- Cricut Brayer tool set
- Tweezers
- Holographic iron-on vinyl
- Sewing machine
- Sewing accessories

These are the steps to take to make leather journal cover using the Cricut machine:

Step 1: On Design Space, open or upload the design

Step 2: Place the leather on the StandardGrip mat, load the mat into the machine and set the machine to cut.

Step 3: On Design Space, open or upload a design to beautify the leather journal cover.

Step 4: Place the iron-on vinyl on the mat, load the mat into the machine and set the machine to it cut out.

Step 5: Weed the iron-on. Burnish the iron-on to stick well to the leather

Step 6: insert the paper journal into the leather cover.

Curving Text for Tumblers

It is necessary to curve the text for tumblers, because they have a conical curve to the surface and not straight. If a straight line of text is used on tumblers, it won't appear straight. Hence, the need to curve the text so that it looks perfect when applied to tumblers.

Tumbler's text templates are already curved and ready to use. However, you need to know how to do it yourself in case you are customizing your own or wish to adjust a template.

The followings steps should be followed when making curving text for tumblers using the Cricut Maker 3:

Step 1: Select the text

Step 2: Use the curve tool and set the diameter to 45 for the text at the top of the tumbler.

For text at the bottom, diameter should be 30.

For text anywhere between the top and the bottom, it varies between 30 – 40 diameter.

Step 3: Cut using the machine.

Step 4: Apply on the tumbler.

You will observe that the text, though curved, will look as if it is straight on the tumbler.

Glass Ornaments with Adhesive vinyl

The materials needed to do make glass ornaments with adhesive vinyl are as follows:

- Adhesive vinyl
- Glass ornaments
- Cricut Maker 3
- Transfer Tape

Use the steps in making vinyl projects here, but note the tips below:

- When placing vinyl on surfaces that are curved, ensure to make the image smaller so that it can adhere better.
- Always place and apply the vinyl from the center and then towards the edges.
- You can use the hair dryer on the adhesive vinyl to make it more flexible when handling.

- Restrain from pressing the glass ornaments too hard, they may break.

Cricut Infusible Ink Mousepad

Follow the steps below to make Cricut Infusible mousepad:

Step 1: Cut your design from the infusible ink sheet, ensuring that your hands are clean and dry.

Step 2: The next thing is to weed away the excess.

Step 3: Cover the EasyPress mat with white cardstock and place it on your mousepad. Put the weeded sheet in place and tape it down to be firm.

Step 4: Place the butcher paper on the design and use the EasyPress to press.

Step 5: Wait for it to cool, and then remove the design from the mousepad to see the result.

FAQs

Is Design Space the same for all Cricut models?

- Yes.

What are the weight and dimensions of the Cricut Maker 3?

- Weight: 4.84 kg (10.68 lbs.)
- Height: 15.06 cm (5.93 in)
- Length: 53.80 cm (21.18 in)

- Depth: 17.75 cm (6.99 in)

There is a USB port in my Cricut Maker 3, what is it for?

- It is for connection with mobile devices to work with the machine. It also charges them.

What is the maximum size I can cut for various materials?

- **Smart Vinyl** – 11.7 in x 12 ft (29.7 cm x 3.6 m)
- **Smart Iron** – 11.7 in x 4 ft (29.7 cm x 1.2 m)
- **Smart Paper Sticker Cardstock** - 11.7" x 11.2" (29.7 cm x 28.4 cm)
- **Smart Paper Sticker Cardstock on a 12" x 12" mat (30.5 cm x 30.5 cm)** – 11.5 " x 11.5 " (29.2 cm x 29.2 cm)
- **Smart Paper Sticker Cardstock on a 12" x 24" mat (30.5 cm x 61 cm)** – 11.5 " x 23.5" (29.2 cm x 59.6 cm)

Is the power adapter of Cricut Maker 3 the same as that of Cricut Explore 3?

- No, the power adapter for Cricut Maker 3 has the output of 3 Amps output while Explore machines have 2,5 Amps. This makes Cricut Maker 3 very powerful that while it is cutting, it can also be charging your smartphone at the same time.

  It is recommended that you use the power adapter of your machine and not use another with it.

Does Cricut Maker 3 have Fast Mode like Cricut Maker?

- Yes. The Cricut Maker 3 is by default on fast mode. It cuts faster and efficiently.

What is the Adaptive Tool System in the Cricut Maker 3?

- The Adaptive Tool system in the Cricut Maker 3 allows for intelligent and efficient use of the mechanism of the rotary blade for precise cut of even the most intricate designs.

Can other brands of iron on or vinyl be used without a mat?

- No. A cutting mat is recommended when using other brands of vinyl or iron-on. Only use Cricut Smart materials without a mat.

Like other materials, can I measure and cut Cricut Smart Materials before loading it to the machine?

- Cricut Materials do not need to be pre-cut before use.

What measurement of Smart Material will be sufficient to cut without a mat?

- 13" x 6" (33 cm x 15.2 cm) minimum

CONCLUSION

As you must have noticed throughout this guide, Cricut Maker 3 is a powerful cutting machine and a crafter's sweetheart. It is used for diverse crafting projects either in school, at home as a hobby or for a small handicraft business.

Cricut Maker 3 can cut more than 300 materials and cuts 10 times faster than the former fast-selling Cricut Explore Air 2. It has several tools to enable you to cut, write, score, embellish and apply decorative items on your projects.

It also has a simple software, Design Space, which has thousands of design templates to pick from and use.

Let's look at the cons and pros of the Cricut Maker 3 to conclude.

The Pros

Cricut has the adaptive tools System that helps in accommodating different types of blades. With the QuickSwap Housing system, the housing does not need to be changed. This will save money, as just the blades need to be replaced at some point.

Design Space, the software to use with Cricut Machine, is a very good resource for vast numbers of ready-to-make designs. It is also very easy to use. The app on portable devices also makes things easy as you can use it on the go.

Cricut Maker 3's capability to work with over 300 materials, including the Smart Materials that do not need cutting mat, is a big thump up for the machine.

The Cons

The Cricut Maker 3 weighs 10.3 kg (22.7 lbs) which makes it heavy and might not be as portable as you would want it to be. However, the weight is understandable considering that it is built to be the most powerful Cricut machine today.

As wonderful as Design Space software is, it is not a complete designing software. It has basic design tools, but you might need to make use of other design software, such as Photoshop, to design some special designs on your own, and then upload them into Design Space.

Design Space is mainly used with Internet connection. If you have no Internet connection or the network is poor in your area, you will not be able to complete your cutting projects to meet your deadline.

Finally, Cricut Maker 3 is not your average inexpensive machine. It sells at about $400 and you need to budget to buy additional tools and materials, because only samples of materials come with the box.

ABOUT THE AUTHOR

Estefana Smith is an artist, craft maker and a writer. She loves to draw and make handcrafts, which she in turn shares in her writing. She has written several articles and books on several craft topics.

When Estefana is not crafting, drawing or writing, she enjoys cycling, reading books about handcrafts, baking and strolling. She lives in Palo Alto with her husband and three kids.

Manufactured by Amazon.ca
Bolton, ON